A CONCEPTUAL THEORY OF RHETORIC

Frank J. D'Angelo

Arizona State University

Winthrop Publishers, Inc.

Cambridge, Massachusetts

Library of Congress Cataloging in Publication Data

D'Angelo, Frank J
  A conceptual theory of rhetoric.

  Bibliography: p.
  1. Rhetoric. I. Title.
  PN187.D3   808   74-32007
  ISBN 0-87626-134-9

To my wife, Sylvia

and

To my children

This book is affectionately dedicated

CONTENTS

PREFACE

Rhetoric is concerned primarily with linguistic and rhetorical principles and with the forms of discourse. This point of view, I think, is implicit in classical rhetoric although the kinds of principles and forms may have differed slightly from those with which we are familiar today. We get a hint of this division of rhetoric into principles and forms in Quintilian's *Institutio Oratoria* (III. III-IV). In discussing the kinds (forms) of oratory, Quintilian observed that commentators in his day confused the "parts" of rhetoric with the "kinds" of rhetoric. By the parts of rhetoric, Quintilian was referring to the traditional division of rhetoric into invention, arrangement, style, memory, and delivery. By the kinds of rhetoric, he meant the three kinds of oratory: the laudative, the deliberative, and the judicial. The former, Quintilian maintained, refer to the "art" of rhetoric, whereas the latter refer to the kinds of material. Each "kind" of oratory contains the whole of discourse, for each uses the principles of invention, arrangement, style, memory, and delivery.

By linguistic principles of rhetoric, I mean those that can be found in the major linguistic texts: syntactic principles, morphological principles, phonological and graphological principles, and semantic principles. By rhetorical principles, I mean those of invention, arrangement, style, memory, and delivery, although there are undoubtedly many more. The forms of discourse are those enumerated by Alexander Bain (narration, description, exposition, persuasion, poetry) or more recently those delineated by James Kinneavy in *A Theory of Discourse* (expressive, persuasive, literary, referential). Considerations of writer, purpose, and audience are related to the modes of discourse.

The theory proposed in this book is concerned almost exclusively with the linguistic and rhetorical (or, as I term them, "conceptual") principles of rhetoric. These principles pertain to the fundamental laws, rules, and conventions of discourse. They determine the intrinsic nature of discourse, as opposed to the forms of discourse which are extrinsic in relation to the nature of discourse. So, for example, a linguistic principle such as coordination or a rhetorical principle such as cause and effect may be found in any form of discourse. *The principles inform the forms.*

This book attempts to explore the relationships that exist between thinking and writing, within the framework of a coherent theoretical system of rhetoric. Its principal features might be described as follows:

1. Invention, arrangement, and style are connected to each other and to underlying thought processes in important ways.
2. The process of invention continues throughout the composing process.
3. The topics of invention are symbolic manifestations of underlying thought processes, and they are essentially relational.
4. Nonlogical thought processes are important in the composing process.
5. The composing process is holistic and organic.
6. The composing process is a movement from an undifferentiated whole to a differentiated whole and repeats in microcosm larger evolutionary processes.
7. The overall shape of a discourse is more important than its parts.
8. Form consciousness is essential to good writing.
9. Syntagmatic and paradigmatic analyses of structure in discourse can be useful in developing a sense of form consciousness and in producing discourse.
10. Rhetoric is by its very nature interdisciplinary. Therefore, studies in cognitive psychology, psychoneurology, psychotherapy, linguistics, psycholinguistics, and anthropology, for example, may contribute important insights to the study of rhetoric.

Chapter I provides a general introduction to the study of rhetoric and to the revival of rhetoric. Chapter II discusses the importance of structure in other disciplines, in thinking, and in discourse. Chapter III places the theory of rhetoric in the context of other theories and then delineates the essential characteristics of this theory. Chapter IV deals with memory, the commonplaces, and with the logical and nonlogical topics of invention. Chapters V and VI proceed both deductively and inductively. The deductive movement ties in the concept of arrangement to that of invention. The inductive movement illustrates the nature of syntagmatic and paradigmatic differentiation. Chapter VII deals with the relationship between style and arrangement. Chapter VIII suggests ways in which interdisciplinary inquiry might go and enumerates some of the unsolved problems in the field.

Implicit in any theory of rhetoric is a world view. The antecedents of this theory lie in the classical world view of the Greeks, who perceived the universe as being essentially ordered and harmonious, following universal forms, laws, and principles. Form in discourse, according to this view, is simply a manifestation of a larger forming agent or principle in the universe. The modern world view is essentially organic and holistic. Its metaphors are for the most part taken from biology or ecology. It sees the universe as a unity, connected, always in process, and moving toward an intelligible goal. The composing process mirrors this movement toward intelligible structure.

The universe is characterized by intelligence, by design, and by interdependence. But this intelligence is not only manifested by logical processes. Therefore, it is necessary to combine the scientific views of Aristotle or Teilhard de Chardin with the metaphysical views of Plato, Jung, Maslow, and Assagioli, to achieve a new synthesis.

The idea that we are in the midst of a revolution in consciousness is an idea that is becoming increasingly more evident in our culture today. Some scholars see it as essentially a romantic revolution and suggest that the anti-rationalistic, counter-cultural movement of the sixties is a harbinger of the new consciousness. But more comprehensive thinkers such as Aldous Huxley, Teilhard de Chardin, Erich Neumann, and Roberto Assagioli see it as the birth of a superconsciousness in which the rational and intuitive elements in the universe are harmonized into one grand design.

Any new rhetoric, therefore, should take into account these larger views. Any new rhetoric should focus on logical and nonlogical modes of thought, on reason and imagination, on thinking and feeling, on linearity and holism, on personal writing as well as on expository and persuasive writing. Any new rhetoric should be a rhetoric not just of the age of technology, but of the Cosmic Age.

I wish to thank Professors Richard L. Larson of the City University of New York, Edward P. J. Corbett of Ohio State University, Robert Gorrell of the University of Nevada, W. Ross Winterowd of the University of Southern California, James Kinneavy of the University of Texas, and Jerome Archer of Arizona State University for reading and offering constructive criticism on various parts of the manuscript. I also wish to thank Professor Wilfred A. Ferrell of Arizona State University for his encouragement of this project and Professor Leslie T. Whipp of the University of Nebraska at Lincoln, whose influence permeates every part of this book. In addition, I would like to thank David Grady of Goodyear Publishing Co. for his early encouragement of my work and Paul O'Connell of Winthrop Publishers, Inc. for his generous help and support. I am also indebted to Sharon Bryan and Nancy Benjamin of Winthrop Publishers for their editorial assistance. Finally, I am particularly grateful to my wife whose patience, daily strength, love, and sacrifices enabled me to complete this book and to persist in all my endeavors.

Much of the research and work on this book was made possible by the generous assistance of the University Grants Committee of Arizona State University.

ACKNOWLEDGMENTS

Ray Billington, "The Frontier Disappears," from *The American Story,* ed. Earl S. Miers. Copyright 1956 by Broadcast Music, Inc. Reprinted with permission of Broadcast Music, Inc.

Carl P. Leubsdorf, "Contrasts Divide Goldwater Race and McGovern's" from *The Arizona Republic* (July 14, 1972). Reprinted with the permission of the Associated Press.

Everett Dean Martin excerpt reprinted from *The Meaning of a Liberal Education* by Everett Dean Martin. By permission of W. W. Norton & Company, Inc. Copyright 1926 by W. W. Norton & Company, Inc. Copyright renewed 1954 by Daphne Mason.

Thomas Wolfe excerpt from *You Can't Go Home Again* by Thomas Wolfe. Copyright 1934, 1937, 1938, 1939, 1940 by Maxwell Perkins as Executor; renewed 1968 by Paul Gitlin. By permission of Harper & Row, Publishers, Inc.

C. L. Wrenn excerpt from *The English Language.* Reprinted by permission of the publisher, Methuen & Co., Ltd.

Part of Chapter V, "Arrangement: Syntagmatic Structure," was published in *College Composition and Communication* (December, 1974) and is reprinted with the permission of NCTE.

Chapter VII, "Style and Structure," was published in *Style* (Spring, 1974) and is reprinted with the permission of *Style.*

I

GENERAL INTRODUCTION

The purpose of this book is to outline a new approach to rhetoric, a conceptual theory of rhetoric which deals with the relationship between thought and discourse. Rhetoric seems to be badly in need of a new organizing principle, a new conceptual framework which will not only relate the old and new in writing, but which will also produce a fairly coherent body of ideas about the nature of the written language. To fulfill this purpose, I will draw in a general way upon cognitive psychology, linguistics, psycholinguistics, and scientific theory, and upon whatever is useful in classical and modern rhetoric. Since I am interested in making composition itself an object of study, at several points I will focus on particular instances of writing to draw some generalizations from them. The gaps in the subject as I treat it here will be far too great for this study to be regarded as a complete theory or even a complete methodology. Rather it is to be considered as a tentative body of generalizations and techniques to be tested and evaluated by rhetoricians, teachers of composition, and students of rhetoric.

Rhetoric Defined

From the time of Aristotle, rhetoric has generally been considered an art. Aristotle himself defined rhetoric as the art of discovering the available means of persuasion in any given case. And since the time of Aristotle, rhetoric has been variously defined as the art of speaking or writing effectively, the art of verbal communication, and the art of effective expression. But what if rhetoric were a science as well as an art? Such a view of rhetoric would change its character from the intuitive (conceived in this sense as the exercising of skills that cannot be learned by study alone), the practical, and the prescriptive to the systematic, the theoretical, and the descriptive. Such a view is certainly implicit in the recent work of those scholars who have attempted to derive principles of rhetoric from the study of style and structure in writing. Such a view is also implicit in Martin Steinmann's distinction between two senses of knowing, knowing *how* and knowing *that,* and the kinds of rhetorical research related to these senses of knowing.

As to the two senses of knowing, Steinmann comments:

In the first sense, a person is said to know something (a language, say) if he possesses a certain ability, if he can perform in certain ways (speak the language). He has knowledge because he knows how to do something. In the second sense, he is said to know something (a language, say) if he possesses either a theory (of grammar and semantics) explaining exercise of a certain ability (speaking the language) or information about some historically given events (certain utterances). He has knowledge because he knows *that* something is the case.[1]

Steinmann's distinction between rhetoric as knowing *how* and as knowing *that* can be conceived of as basically the distinction between rhetoric as art (the ability of a person to write or speak effectively), and rhetoric as science (a theory or body of information about rhetoric).

Of the kinds of rhetorical research Steinmann feels is needed, two kinds are relevant for this particular study: basic rhetorical research and pedagogical rhetorical research. Basic rhetorical research "investigates exercise of rhetorical knowledge in the *first* sense (the knowing *how* sense)—that is, exercise of rhetorical ability—and produces rhetorical knowledge in the *second* sense (the knowing *that* sense)—specifically, theories of rhetoric that, to the extent that they are adequate, explain exercise of rhetorical ability."[2] Pedagogical rhetorical research differs in that it "investigates exercise of pedagogical rhetorical ability—the ability to produce rhetorical ability, to teach oral or written composition—and produces theories of teaching rhetorical ability. Its object is not exercise of rhetorical ability (the object of basic research), but one means of acquisition of it, by formal instruction." [3]

Perhaps an even more useful distinction than that between rhetoric as an art and as a science would be that between rhetoric and composition. Rhetoric, in this view, is a science which attempts to discover general principles of oral or written discourse. It subjects its findings and conclusions to close examination and verification. A rhetorician, therefore, is one who attempts to discover these rhetorical principles. Composition is essentially the art of applying these principles in writing, and the teacher of composition is one who tries to impart some of these principles to his students as well as to give the students a way of arriving at their own ideas about writing.

This study grew out of the recent widespread interest in the revival of classical rhetoric and in the development of new rhetorics. What follows is a consideration of the implications of this revival, with a view toward establishing some sort of coherent framework in which to place this study.

Revival of Rhetoric

The revival of rhetoric has led both to a significant interest in the possibilities of classical rhetoric as well as to a growing interest in the development of new rhetorics. Those who are interested in the revival of classical rhetoric feel that it can still be the basis of a valid approach to writing and that it offers the only complete system of rhetoric which is available to us today. Classical rhetoric is "the system, concerned primarily with persuasive discourse, that was first formulated in fifth century Athens, that flourished in Augustan Rome, that constituted a member of the trivium in medieval schools, that became a dominant force in English education during the Renaissance and remained a prominent part of the curriculum until the first quarter of the nineteenth century." [4] It is the rhetoric of Aristotle, Cicero, and Quintilian. It can be found in such books as Aristotle's *Rhetoric*, Cicero's *De Oratore*, Quintilian's *Institutio Oratoria* and in later works such as Thomas Wilson's *Arte of*

Rhetorique and *Rule of Reason,* Blair's *Lectures on Rhetoric and Belles Lettres* and Richard Whately's *Elements of Rhetoric.*[5] Edward Corbett has succinctly summarized the principal features of this tradition:

> Aristotle's *Rhetoric* was the fountainhead of the system commonly called "classical rhetoric"—a system of rhetoric that dealt primarily with persuasive oratory; that spoke about three kinds of persuasive discourse—the deliberative (the rhetoric of the public assembly), the forensic (the rhetoric of the courtroom) and the epideictic (the rhetoric of ceremonial occasions); that treated of the five parts of rhetoric—invention, arrangement, style, memory, and delivery; that spoke in connection with invention, of the topics as a system for turning up arguments in a given case; that spoke of the three modes of appeal—the appeal to reason, the appeal to emotions, and the appeal of the speaker's character; that dealt with the two basic forms that the logical appeal took— the inductive example and the deductive enthymeme; that spoke, in connection with arrangement, of the parts of a discourse—the exordium or introduction, the narratio or the statement of the situation, the confirmation or proof of one's thesis, the refutation of an opponent's objections, and the epilogue or conclusion; that spoke, in connection with style, of such things as diction, rhythm, schemes, and tropes.[6]

Some scholars, however, feel that the revival of rhetoric must be more than a revival of earlier rhetorics. This point of view is expressed by Wayne Booth, who writes: "It is simply that none of them can possibly give us the comprehensive rhetorical theory we seek. Living in a new kind of rhetorical age, surrounded by, indeed practicing daily forms of persuasion their authors never dreamed of, we inevitably hunger for a theory that will do justice to *our* manifold rhetorical experiences, and we do not find that the categories used by earlier theorists quite do the job."[7] Booth believes that modern grammars, logics, and semantics will be indispensable in any new approach to rhetoric. Richard Young and Alton Becker see inherent weaknesses in traditional rhetoric:

> First, the classical art of invention stresses authoritative confirmation of present beliefs, while modern modes of inquiry stress

imaginative discovery of new facts and relationships. Second, the art of arrangement includes only patterns of persuasion, and neglects consideration of form in other important rhetorical modes such as description, narration, and exposition. Third, both the art of arrangement and the art of style divorce form from content, failing to consider the importance of the act of discovery in the shaping of form. And finally, the art of style is concerned primarily with embellishing, clarifying, and giving point to sentences, an approach which neglects both the deeper personal roots of style and the ways in which style is manifested in patterns beyond the sentence.[8]

Other scholars believe that the best new rhetoric will be one which somehow shares in the tradition of old rhetoric. In this regard, Joseph Schwartz comments: "I look forward to new theories of rhetoric and to the practice of new rhetorics (as artists), but I do not forsee the development of something so new that it cannot be regarded as part of the tradition of rhetoric."[9] Similarly, W. Ross Winterowd contends that "because rhetoric does not and cannot have an autonomous subject matter, it cannot make a dramatic departure that will leave the old behind. But this statement does not mean that new theory and practice cannot accrue to it, thus, in effect, bringing about a revision to make the subject meaningful—even vital—for the here-and-now."[10] Finally, Edward Corbett makes a plea for a variety of approaches to rhetoric: "I see," he writes, "exciting possibilities in the new rhetorics and the new stylistics that are beginning to form all about us. But I see much of proven value in the old rhetoric too."[11]

In any discussion of new rhetorics, a variety of names and positions is sure to appear. Among these are the work done by Francis Christensen with the rhetoric of the sentence and the paragraph (*Notes Toward a New Rhetoric*); the theory of rhetoric developed by Richard Young, Alton Becker, and Kenneth Pike, based on tagmemic theory (*Rhetoric: Discovery and Change*); and the approach to discourse theory being developed by James Kinneavy (*A Theory of Discourse*). Others mentioned as possible contributors to new rhetorics are Chaim Perelman, Stephen Toulmin, Richard Weaver, Kenneth Burke, I. A. Richards, Marshall McLuhan, Noam Chomsky, and B. F. Skinner.

The implication of the revival of interest in classical rhetoric and the possibilities of new rhetorics, then, seems to be that no significant new rhetoric can emerge *ab nihilo*. No new rhetoric, for example, can afford to neglect the rhetorical concepts of invention, arrangement, and style, or such traditional basic concerns as the relationship of the writer to his purpose, his subject, and his audience. One might conclude that rhetoric does not necessarily end with Aristotle, but this is no reason why some of the concepts associated with Aristotle cannot be used as a point of departure.

The viewpoint taken in this study is that the best new rhetoric is one that will somehow relate the old and the new in rhetoric. So, for example, a modern theory of invention might start with the topics of Aristotle, but at some point it might also consider the findings of cognitive psychology. A modern theory of arrangement might draw upon current linguistic studies to describe the organizational patterns of modern prose. But we need to have more than a grammatical description of patterns of organization; we need to know something about conceptual patterns and about the effect of these patterns in modern discourse. More importantly, we need to relate the processes of invention and arrangement in a more significant way. The study of style might draw from the categories of classical rhetoric, but certainly modern linguistic studies will be all important to a discussion of style in any new rhetoric. Further, the study of style might overlap with the study of arrangement. For example, what are the features of style which go beyond the sentence level? How might they best be described? Concerning the conceptual patterns that exist in extended discourse, how are these made manifest on the sentence level? Another consideration deals with the art of memory. Is the art of memory obsolete for modern purposes, or can it perhaps be reintegrated in a modern theory of rhetoric?

Clearly, we have barely touched upon the possible concerns of a new rhetoric. For example, the investigation of structure in discourse might lead to an investigation of structure in thought. What is the relationship between thought and language, and what can we learn from studies in cognitive psychology, perception theory, psycholinguistics, or anthropology that will possibly illuminate this relationship? The analysis of thought has preoccupied rhetoricians and grammarians in previous ages. How important are these ideas today? It seems that anyone interested in developing a new approach to rhetoric must go outside his field to consider recent studies in linguistics, semantics, psychology, and literary criticism, to name just a few areas of interdisciplinary concern. How can we intelligently use the findings in these fields for the study of rhetoric?

The subject of this study, then, is a conceptual theory of rhetoric. The intent is to investigate the possible relationships that obtain between thought and discourse, to relate them to the traditional concerns of classical rhetoric, and to suggest one direction that an emerging new theory of rhetoric might take, as well as to offer a methodology and some generalizations about rhetoric which might be useful to scholars, teachers, and students of rhetoric. An additional purpose is to provide some badly needed basic rhetorical and pedagogical research by focusing upon specific examples of extended discourse.

Notes

1. Martin Steinmann, Jr., ed., "Rhetorical Research," *New Rhetorics* (New York: Charles Scribner's Sons, 1967), p. 18.

2. Steinmann, p. 23.

3. Steinmann, pp. 25–26.

4. Edward P. J. Corbett, "A New Look at Old Rhetoric," *Rhetoric: Theories for Application,* ed. Robert Gorrell (Champaign, Ill.: National Council of Teachers of English, 1967), p. 17.

5. Albert Duhamel, "Traditional Misconceptions of Traditional Rhetoric," *Rhetoric: Theories for Application,* ed. Robert Gorrell (Champaign, Ill.: National Council of Teachers of English, 1967), p. 23.

6. Edward P. J. Corbett, "What Is Being Revived?" *College Composition and Communication,* XVIII (October 1967), 166–167.

7. Wayne C. Booth, "The Revival of Rhetoric," *New Rhetorics,* ed. Martin Steinmann, Jr. (New York: Charles Scribner's Sons, 1967), p. 12.

8. Richard E. Young and Alton L. Becker, "Toward a Modern Theory of Rhetoric: A Tagmemic Contribution," *New Rhetorics,* ed. Martin Steinmann, Jr. (New York: Charles Scribner's Sons, 1967), p. 85.

9. Joseph Schwartz, "Kenneth Burke, Aristotle, and the Future of Rhetoric," *College Composition and Communication,* XVII (December 1966), 215.

10. W. Ross Winterowd, *Rhetoric: A Synthesis* (New York: Holt, Rinehart and Winston, Inc., 1968), p. 78.

11. Corbett, "A New Look at Old Rhetoric," p. 22.

II

STRUCTURE

Because the concept of structure (and its obvious analogs *form, figure, shape, design, type, outline, pattern, plan, design, archetype*) is such an important one for the theory and practice of rhetoric and because in subsequent chapters I will be making specific connections between this concept and the study of rhetoric, I would like to discuss at some length the importance of structure in general, its significance in various fields, and its value for the study of structure in rhetoric.

Importance of Structure

The notion of structure is a central concept of our time, writes Gyorgy Kepes, in his introduction to *Structure in Art and Science*. Every era, Kepes declares, looks for a controlling metaphor, a model for understanding the world of man and nature. The concept of structure is our model of understanding, and it is not inaccurate to separate the idea of structure from the concept of content. Kepes continues:

> The most powerful imaginative vision is structure-oriented. As old connections crumble away, inevitably our creative efforts seek out new ordering principles to replace the old. In different fields, for different reasons, the new ordering relations are being accepted as fundamental. Scientists, for example, have come to recognize that

9

the key properties of different materials are determined according to the way in which atoms, the basic building units of nature, are arrayed and the way in which they are joined together, rather than, as was once assumed, according to the elemental stuff of the material. The differences among solid, liquid, and gaseous states are explained by the patterning of their atoms, the relative closeness of their molecules.

From inorganic structures to plants and animals, from the movement of animals to their social behavior patterns and to human relations, structure is central. Inherent in the spiral structure of the complex molecule DNA is the ability to reproduce life itself. Thus, a built-in program of growth and development is provided for an infinite variety of unfolding structures of living forms.

Structure is also central to our understanding of our ways of understanding. Studies of our perceptual and cognitive processes by Gestalt psychologists show that psychological events do not occur through the accumulation of individual elements of sense data but through the coordinated functioning of clearly patterned networks of sensation determined by structural laws.[1]

Kepes's view is shared by Lancelot L. Whyte, who writes:

During this century the attention of scientists has been moving from the simple towards the complex, with the result that a modern conception of STRUCTURE is, for some purposes, replacing the older conceptions of ATOMISM and of FORM. The unifying natural philosophy of the coming period may be a morphology, a doctrine of form viewed as structure. There is a shift of emphasis from relatively isolated small units and over-all shapes, towards a single comprehensive and precise identification of structural patterns and their changes. Arrangement, configuration, organization, structure, ordering—these are now key words. What underlies this verbal fashion? Greater attention to complexity.[2]

Order, arrangement, structure—these concepts seem to be a necessary precondition in order for the mind to be able to understand anything.

Without order the world of experience becomes a shapeless mass. Music becomes mere noise; a painting becomes a blob of paint; a play becomes a happening. The human mind, the order of nature, social organizations, art, the solar system—all dissolve in a chaos of particles. The idea of order seems to be deeply rooted in the human condition. It would be difficult, perhaps impossible, to find objects and events which do not reflect some signs of an underlying order. The houses that we live in display some sort of spatial order. The streets of our cities reveal planning of some kind. The displays of food in our supermarkets exhibit a pattern of arrangement. The cycle of the seasons and the movement of the planets clearly proclaim that nature is orderly. If there is order in nature, is it not one of the tasks of scholars in various fields to discover that order? In science and in art, the search for structures is increasing in order to account for the complexity of nature. May not the present embarrassment of rhetoric, the dearth of new ideas, the lack of interest in composition by our best scholars, be due to the neglect of structure? It is important to rhetoric that we look for a new formative principle, a simple order, to bring a new unity to the study of rhetoric. Perhaps the study of structure will provide that unity.

The new interest in structure replaces the older interest in atomism, which reduces complex data to discrete entities. Most physical systems display definite patterns of arrangement in which the individual particles are indistinguishable except to sophisticated instruments. The pattern is more important than the individual constituents; the function of the individual constituents seems to be to build up the patterns. In many different fields, interest has shifted from a concern with discrete parts and with surface appearances to an interest in the total pattern and the underlying structure. In psychology, in biology, in chemistry, in physics, in linguistics, in modern art, the old interest in atomism is being replaced by a newer interest in structure. As these concerns relate to rhetoric, could it not be said that the old rhetoric spoke mainly of particles (words, sentences, paragraphs, outlines), while the new rhetoric must learn to speak of systems, patterns, orders, of complex arrangements of structures of different kinds?

In more and more fields, a knowledge of structure is considered to be fundamental. Structure is central to the understanding and appreciation of artistic expression. For example, it is the structure of a literary work, its formal characteristics, which partly determines its quality as literature. Perception of the formal patterns in a literary work is basic to our appreciation of its aesthetic effectiveness. Various approaches to literary criticism seem to reflect this concern with structure in different ways. Thus the New Critics occupied themselves with the structures of irony and paradox in a literary work, the Neo-Aristotelian critics with plot structures and genres, and the Archetypal critics with archetypal patterns of plot and imagery. Structure is also important in our understanding and appreciation of pictorial form. Color, texture, design, balance, contrast, symmetry—all are elements in a painting that make up its structural complexity and that are so important in our perception of its effectiveness. Abstract painting, especially cubism and nonrepresentational art, it seems to me, is concerned with the search for significant structures. Unlike the artists of the Renaissance, many modern artists are searching for forms and shapes which have more in common with microscopic organic and nonorganic systems found in science than they do with familiar, everyday shapes and forms.

In recent years, more and more scholars have become interested in the structural properties of language as distinct from its meaning. For example, structural linguists such as Charles Fries have attempted to describe the structural patterns of sentences aside from whatever meaning these sentences might have. This does not mean that every type of semantic meaning has been excluded from linguistic studies. Rather it indicates that more and more attention is being given to structure, to contrastive differences in the formal arrangements of structural patterns, structural cues and signals, and the formal arrangements of the functioning units. Transformational linguists such as Noam Chomsky have concerned themselves with the formal qualities of language, but in a different way. According to the transformationalist view, a grammar has three components: a syntactical component, a semantic component, and a phonological component. The syntactical component is primary; it is a kind of abstract string of structural entities to which the other two components adhere. The semantic component assigns a semantic interpretation to syntactic structures; the phonological component assigns a phonetic interpretation to syntactic structures. Since everything is mediated through the syntactic component, it is evident that syntactic structure is fundamental to our understanding of English sentences. Despite the differences in general approach and point of view, both structural linguists and transformationalists are interested in structure, form, arrangement, shape, in all of those formal characteristics of language which are distinct from its sound qualities or its meaning.

Form consciousness seems to be a fundamental concern of scholars in many different disciplines. Yet we seem to have barely touched upon its possibilities for the study of rhetoric. Linguistic analysis of the sentence and of the paragraph has already yielded important insights for the study of rhetoric. And just as linguists have pointed out that the unit of communication in English is not the word, but clusters of words, including meaning-bearing words and signal words, so also it may be that individual sentences or paragraphs function only in combinations and that rhetorical units should be studied in clusters. Patterns of discourse larger than the sentence or the paragraph are structurally describable, and these patterns can be approached by means of a descriptive analysis. If the ability to perceive form is so basic to our understanding of sentences and paragraphs, how much more important it must be for our understanding of extended units of discourse. Organization is of the utmost importance in all good writing, and the best writers are usually those who can perceive form in their own writing. Unfortunately, the traditional concepts of unity and coherence have not been very helpful in this regard. More rhetorical research is needed to develop concepts that will be useful in the analysis of the structure of extended units of discourse.

I have said that linguistics can offer a system of analysis which will enable us to perceive form in discourse. It is probable that new insights derived from such disciplines as anthropology, psycholinguistics, psychology, and biology will be equally important in the study of form consciousness and in suggesting new ways of understanding and organizing discourse. For example, possibilities exist in the field of psychology for relating the structure of thinking to the structure of writing. Psychologists, like researchers in other fields, are moving away from a narrow concern with atomism, to a broader concern with structure.

Structure in Thinking

Many contemporary psychologists consider thought to be a structural process, but it is the gestalt psychologists, more than any others, who make this assumption explicit. According to gestalt psychology, we do not perceive just stimuli, but *patterns* of stimuli. Perception is of the whole. This is so because the human organism imposes wholeness upon the elements of perception. As external stimuli impinge upon the organism, neural activities in the organism induce states of consciousness that organize energies within the viewer. These energies then manifest themselves in a structuring of the environment. Stimulus elements lend themselves to patterning for a number of reasons: because of their near-ness to one another in time and space and because of their similarity. More importantly, however, stimulus elements form complete patterns because the human organism will not tolerate chaos; if forms are incom-plete, then the organism will tend to complete them. Thus the principle of closure is an important aspect of perception. Consciousness, therefore, is not composed of discrete elements of experience, but it is a unified whole.

Perhaps the most explicit formulation of the idea that thinking is structural can be found in the work of Max Wertheimer who writes:

> Thinking consists in
> envisaging, realizing structural features and structural require-ments; proceeding in accordance with and determined by, these requirements; thereby changing the situation in the direction of structural improvements which involves:
> that gaps, trouble-regions, disturbances, superficialities, etc., be viewed and dealt with structurally; that inner structural relations—fitting or not fitting—be sought among disturbances and the given situation as a whole and among its various parts;
> that there be operations of structural groupings and segrega-tion, of centering, etc.;
> that operations be viewed and treated in their structural place, role, dynamic meaning, including realization of the changes which this involves;
> realizing structural transposability, structural hierarchy, and separating structurally peripheral from fundamental features —a special case of grouping;
> looking for structural rather than piecemeal truth.[3]

In Wertheimer's view, the process of thinking begins with an attempt to get at the internal relationships of the object or event to be known. This involves a knowledge of how the parts are related to the whole; it in-volves a kind of logical hierarchy of all of the parts. The ways in which these parts are connected is not arbitrary. Each part performs a particular structural function; each is consistent and reasonable in its place in the whole. The emphasis is on functional meaning, on dynamic interrelationships.

The view that thinking is structural is also shared by some nongestalt psychologists. Piaget, for example, contends that "intelligence, viewed as a whole, takes the form of a structuring which impresses certain patterns on the interaction between the subject or subjects and near or distant surrounding objects. Its originality resides essentially in the nature of the patterns that it constructs to this effect." [4] Intelligence, according to Piaget, consists of the sum total of cognitive processes. It includes perception, habit, and sensory–motor activities. Intelligence is not a faculty; it is a form of equilibrium towards which all of the so-called higher forms of thought as well as the lower forms of cognition tend. All of these forms of behavior display some kind of structuring. Thus instinct manifests itself in patterning; habit and perception evidence patterning; intuitive thought as well as formal thought reveal patterning; and underlying all of these structures of mental life, linking them all together, may be found rhythmic patterns: hunger, thirst, the sexual appetites, periodic behavior, walking, movement in general.[5]

One of the most important of these rhythmic patterns is that related to auditory memory. Research has indicated that if a subject is asked to remember a series of, say, eight digits, these digits are stored and recalled more easily if the subject groups them into patterns. Thus the series "72853916" is more easily remembered if it is grouped as "728-539-16." For some reason, other groupings such as "7285-3916" will not do as well. Apparently this particular sequence is a single structural unit with a rhythmic pattern that can be easily recalled. Evidently the subject intuitively *creates* this rhythmic pattern and incorporates it into his active memory by repeating the rhythmic pattern that he creates and subsequently hears. We all know how much easier it is to recall a rhythmic pattern if it is short and if we repeat it often. Counting-out rhymes are a good case in point: here the rhythmic pattern serves as a sequence of cues and as a support for what is to be remembered.[6] This approach to auditory memory has much in common with the gestalt approach to perception. (The rhythmic pattern, like a gestalt, is a configuration which we create whenever we try to remember.) It offers additional evidence for the importance of structure in all of the cognitive processes.

If, as the evidence seems to indicate, intelligence manifests structuring of some kind, then these psychological processes (according to some psychologists) must have their counterparts in underlying physiological processes in the brain. (Others would argue that these structures, though latent, are not fully formed, but become more clearly distinct as structures by being used.)

> To gestalt psychologists, there is an identity of form (hence, "isomorphism") between psychological or conscious processes and their underlying physiological processes. . . . In other words, isomorphism considers that there is a fundamental and invariable relationship between physiological and conscious aspects of behavior. . . . psychology seeks to understand and explain the conscious aspect of experience, while inferring that the physiological aspect has an identical form. It would relate the two by proving, in instance after instance, that they *do* have the same form.[7]

As these ideas relate to the study of form and structure in rhetoric, can we extrapolate further? If, for example, we can infer the existence of underlying physiological processes from conscious aspects of behavior, can we not go one step more and assume that there is a direct relationship, perhaps an isomorphism, between the products of these conscious processes and underlying mental processes? In other words, conceptual thinking often manifests itself in symbols: in words, in images, or in numbers. Can we not infer from these symbol systems corresponding symbolic, operational, or perceptual activities in the brain? More specifically as it relates to rhetoric, the verbal pattern symbolizes the logical operation. Implicit therefore in any pattern of discourse are the mental processes that the writer had to perform to arrive at that pattern of discourse. These patterns of discourse we call "conceptual patterns of discourse" because they relate to the operational activities of conceptualizing. Thus from the existence of conceptual patterns in discourse, we infer the existence of similar patterns of thought; from the existence of conceptual patterns of thought, we can infer the existence of corresponding patterns in discourse. One of the tasks of the rhetorician is to relate the structure of thought to the structure of discourse.

The Structure of Discourse

For some time now, rhetoricians have been pointing out the need for relating the structure of discourse to the processes of thinking, but for the most part they have gone unheeded. As early as 1963, for example, Robert Gorrell maintained that the "investigation of structure in thought seems . . . necessary to understanding structure in language and to understanding principles of rhetoric. . . . it is useful to explore the structure of thought as a basis for describing the structure of language . . . because in various ways language and thought are connected and we need to know how." [8] Dudley Bailey reiterated this idea a short time later, amplifying it and suggesting a possible new direction. The task of modern rhetoric, according to Bailey, is to "undertake to show, as systematically as may be, the sorts of relations which obtain among the details of our thought—obtain successfully, that is, in educated discourse. In other words —what are the logical and psychological patterns which listeners and readers of our language understand, and indeed anticipate, in our discourse? And to what extent can we explain their logical and psychological grounds and illustrate them for the student?" [9]

> There are clearly recognized patterns in time, and fictional techniques utilize them commonly. There are also clearly recognized patterns in space, and descriptive writers use them. . . . then there are logical patterns. From the logical conventions of induction we derive the patterns of "details" and of "illustrations." . . . From the logical conventions of categorization, we derive the patterns of definition and "logical analysis"; from logical conventions of analogy we derive the patterns of comparison and contrast; from the logical conventions of causation we derive the patterns of hypothesis. From psychological conventions we derive such patterns as those of repetition and various kinds of "impressionism." [10]

More recently, Les Whipp has called for the study of extended units of discourse which would combine "both a concern for grammatical relationships transcending the limits of the sentence (a concern sometimes of recent tagmemic grammar) and a concern for conceptual or meaning relationships which transcend the sentence (a concern sometimes of recent British philosophy)." [11] Francis Christensen has done extensive work on the rhetoric of the paragraph. But few scholars in recent years have attempted to describe conceptual relationships and structures in discourse beyond the paragraph.

By conceptual patterns of discourse I mean verbal patterns related to thinking activity. These patterns are symbol systems which are objectively distinct from thinking, yet which refer directly to it. They are conceptual because they relate to the notion of thinking in concepts. They are related to the categories of classical rhetoric and of traditional logic (definition, analysis, classification, and the like); they are related to the "laws" of classical association theory (contiguity, similarity, repetition, association); they are related to the categories of Kant (time, space, substance, causation, unity, identity, resemblance, difference); the abstract relations of Peter Roget (existence, relation, quantity, order, number, time, change, causation); they are related to the patterns of experience of Kenneth Burke. They are logical and psychological, spatial and temporal. They are all about us, but the problem for the rhetorician is to gather them up, analyze them closely, and point out more precisely than has been done in the past exactly how they relate to thought processes and to the concerns of rhetoric. So, for example, the process of "abstraction" is an important mental operation, but it would be difficult to relate it directly to a pattern of discourse. On the other hand, "comparison" is a mental operation which does correspond to a pattern of discourse. It is also one of the topics of classical rhetoric and it can be related to one of the laws of association in associationist psychology. Some categories will fit, some will not. "Number" is not a pattern of discourse, but "enumeration" is. "Time" is not a pattern of discourse, but "narration," which is related to time, is. "Space" is not a pattern of discourse, but "description," which is related to space, is. To bring these patterns together will require, as Dudley Bailey puts it, "a laborious gathering of eggs." Yet it can be, should be, done.

Inasmuch as rhetoric attempts to discover and to describe grammatical and conceptual patterns in discourse, it is descriptive, in the same way that modern linguistics is descriptive. In fact, one of the main tasks of any new rhetoric is to describe fully, precisely, and clearly the relationships that obtain among extended units of discourse. These relationships include syntactical relationships which extend beyond the limits of the sentence or the paragraph, as well as meaning or conceptual relationships. What are the patterns that inform well-wrought instances of extended discourse? What are the techniques that a writer uses to achieve a meaningful whole? How are the words and sentences arranged in meaningful patterns? What are the rhetorical effects of such patterns? For what purposes can these patterns and techniques be used by other writers? What are the advantages of using one particular pattern over another in different contexts? Although these techniques and patterns may be more numerous than we suppose, surely they are finite and can be subjected to objective analysis and description. Just as linguists have been able to reduce almost all English sentences to a few basic types, perhaps rhetoricians will discover the basic pattern types of extended units of discourse. Many such patterns are already widely known, but we need to identify many more, and we need someone to put them into a meaningful pattern and to discuss their rhetorical implications and applications.

This view assumes that there are formal patterns which recur constantly in oral and written discourse that can be discovered and described and made the basis of rhetorical principles for theory and pedagogy. As Kenneth Burke expressed it:

> You can't possibly make a statement without its falling into some sort of pattern. Its formality can then be abstracted and named, without reference to any particular subject matter, hence can be looked upon as capable of "reindividuation" in a great variety of subject matters. Given enough industry in observation, abstraction, and classification, you can reduce any expression (even inconsequential or incomplete ones) to some underlying skeletal structure.[12]

What is the origin of such forms? Are they innate forms or are they resultant? Clearly, many of these formal patterns can be found in nature and in human experience. Others, such as comparison, contrast, the series, balance, and metaphor, seem to be implicit in the way our minds actually operate. For Burke, it matters not whether these patterns are psychological universals or merely conventional or acquired forms, the idea being that once we have obtained them, they can become the means of organizing discourse. Since Burke's conception of form is so important, I will quote at some length:

There are formal patterns which distinguish our experience. They apply in art, since they apply outside of art. The accelerated motion of a falling body, the cycle of a storm, the gradation of a sunrise, the stages of a cholera epidemic, the ripening of crops—in all such instances we find the material of progressive form. Repetitive form applies to all manner of orientation. . . . Thus, though forms need not be prior to experience, they are certainly prior to the work of art exemplifying them. Psychology and philosophy may decide whether they are innate or resultant; so far as the work of art is concerned they simply are: when one turns to the production or enjoyment of a work of art, a formal equipment is already present, and the effects of art are involved in its utilization. Such ultimate minor forms as contrast, comparison, metaphor, series, bathos, chiasmus, are based upon our modes of understanding anything; they are implicit in the processes of abstraction and generalization by which we think. . . .

Such basic forms may, for all that concerns us, be wholly conventional. The subject–predicate form of sentences, for instance, has sanction enough if we have learned to expect it. It may be "natural" only as a path worn across a field is natural. But if experience has worn a path, the path is there—and in using the path we are obeying the authority of a prior form.[13]

Burke's comments indicate that not only can formal patterns be found in experience, but also that these patterns are exemplified in oral or written discourse. They can thus be abstracted and made the basis of new formal categories and conceptual principles.

As may appear obvious, we have barely touched upon the importance of form and structure for the study of rhetoric. Subsequent chapters, however, will continue to explore the idea of structure in thinking and in discourse and will relate these ideas to some general aspects of theory construction, to the theory of conceptual rhetoric proposed in this study, and to the related concepts of rhetorical invention, arrangement, and style.

Notes

1. Gyorgy Kepes, "Introduction" to *Structure in Art and Science,* ed. Gyorgy Kepes (New York: George Braziller, 1965), pp. ii, iii.

2. Lancelot L. Whyte, "Atomism, Structure, and Form" in *Structure in Art and Science,* ed. Gyorgy Kepes (New York: George Braziller, 1965), p. 20.

3. Max Wertheimer, *Productive Thinking,* Enlarged Edition, ed. Michael Wertheimer (New York: Harper & Brothers, Publishers, 1959), pp. 235–236.

4. Jean Piaget, *The Psychology of Intelligence,* trans. Malcolm Piercy and D. E. Berlyne (London: Routledge & Kegan Paul Ltd., 1947), p. 167.

5. Piaget, pp. 6–7, 167–169.

6. Ulric Neisser, *Cognitive Psychology* (New York: Appleton, 1967), pp. 232–233.

7. W. Edgar Vinacke, *The Psychology of Thinking* (New York: McGraw–Hill Book Co., Inc., 1952), p. 30.

8. Robert M. Gorrell, "Structure in Thought," *College English,* XXIV (May 1963), 592–594.

9. Dudley Bailey, "A Plea for a Modern Set of Topoi," *College English,* XXVI (November 1964), 114.

10. Bailey, pp. 114–115.

11. Leslie T. Whipp, "The Language of Rhetoric," *College Composition and Communication,* XIX (February 1968), 19.

12. Kenneth Burke, *A Rhetoric of Motives* (New York: Prentice–Hall, Inc., 1950), p. 65.

13. Kenneth Burke, *Counter-Statement,* 2nd ed. (Los Altos, California: Hermes Publications, 1953), pp. 141–142.

III

THEORY

There is no magic formula for producing a theory of discourse or, for that matter, for generating any kind of scientific theory. The theorist begins by noticing either the lack of explanatory principles in a particular field or the unsatisfactory nature of existing principles in that field. It is usually a field in which at least some facts, some ideas, some regularities, some generalizations, however crude they may be, have already been established. But the theorist feels a need to bring all of these detached, separate facts and generalizations into a coherent framework. So he looks about for a conceptual scheme, a working hypothesis, a controlling metaphor to explain facts that previously appeared to be unrelated. As Stephen Pepper so concisely phrases it:

A man desiring to understand the world looks about for a clue to its comprehension. He pitches upon some area of common sense fact and tries if he cannot understand other areas in terms of this one. This original area becomes then his basic analogy or root metaphor. He describes as best he can the characteristics of this area, or, if you will, discriminates its structure. A list of its structural characteristics becomes his basic concepts of explanation and description. We call them a set of categories. In terms of these categories he proceeds to study all other areas of fact whether uncriticized or previously criticized. He undertakes to interpret all facts in terms of these categories. As a result of the impact of these other facts upon his categories, he may qualify and readjust the categories, so that a set of categories commonly changes and develops. Since the basic analogy or root metaphor normally (and probably at least in part necessarily) arises out of common sense, a great deal of development and refinement of a set of categories is required if they are to prove adequate for a hypothesis of unlimited scope.[1]

This desire for explanations is the distinctive basis of scientific theories. It leads to an attempt to establish general laws and to assign a structural description to these laws. It is a principal means of ordering experience.

Once the theorist arrives at his working hypotheses, his controlling metaphor, he must put them into a logical framework or formal system so that the basic concepts and categories of his hypothesis can be clearly delineated and meaningfully related to empirical data. There is general agreement among scientific theorists as to the nature of this logical framework.[2] The logical structure of a scientific theory is a formal or semiformal deductive system which consists of a series of two kinds of connected sentences or propositions. The first group of sentences constitutes the hypotheses of the theory. These are the basic premises, the postulates, the axioms of the system. They contain the basic ideas and assumptions of the theory. The second group of sentences follows logically from the first; they are the deduced propositions, the theorems of the deductive system. The ideas they contain are often statements about the relationships that obtain among the concepts of the postulates, or they may be slightly different ideas derived from the postulates.

Together these propositions present a picture or model of the reality that they are supposed to represent. Such a model enables the theorist to organize the data of experience in a significant way, and to choose what appears to be the data relevant to specific purposes; not just any data will do. It enables the researcher to stand off from the discrete aspects of experience and to see them as a logical whole, to infer relationships, to interpret the data, and to make predictions. Theoretical models may be organizational or research-generating, anticipatory or predictive. Ideally, they will be useful not only in enabling us to understand one large segment of reality, but also in generating new ideas and insights, and they may even lead to further hypotheses.

A theory then is not put together from empirical data alone. A theory is what makes it possible for someone to make empirical data intelligible. After the theory is completed, that is the time for empirical testing; at that time there should be some sort of empirical evidence for the hypotheses. Otherwise these hypotheses would be closed to proof or refutation. At the very least, there should be some sort of correlation between the observable facts and the constructs of the logical system.

Thus far we have briefly considered the characteristics of theories in general. But since a theory of discourse must of necessity deal with language, it might be useful to relate this theory of discourse not only to theories in general, but also to linguistic theory, since discourse theory and linguistic theory must, at the very least, share certain assumptions about the nature of language and must connect with each other at various points.

Linguistic Theory

A major branch of modern linguistic theory derives primarily from the work of Noam Chomsky.[3] According to Chomsky, a linguistic theory is not merely a set of procedures which would enable a researcher to accurately analyze and describe English sentences, since a theory of language cannot be reduced to a collection of sentences. A linguistic theory is rather a formal model or system which attempts to offer a logical explanation for the way that language operates. It attempts to show the logical relationships that exist among the sentences of a language as well as to provide a generalized explanation of these relationships. Given a theory of language, the linguist can use it as a model or framework to organize particular sentences of the language. This model or framework consists of a number of generalizations (linguistic universals) which can account for the facts and properties of all languages.

A theory of language therefore is a theory about linguistic universals. This view of language assumes that there are underlying principles which are common to all languages. These principles consist of an innate system of rules which determine, to some extent, the features of particular languages. Although particular languages differ in many ways, linguistic research is continually discovering the many similarities that exist among them. However, these similarities are often obscured because of superficial syntactic differences. The transformational linguist accounts for these superficial differences by postulating various levels of structure:

surface structures, intermediate structures, and deep structures. It is in the deep structure that linguistic universals exist. The deep structure is an abstract formal structure which underlies all sentences and which contains the full meaning of those sentences. Intermediate structures are those structures which mediate between deep and surface structures in accordance with various transformations. Surface structures are the observable forms of sentences, the written or spoken forms which appear after all transformations take place. The sentences of all natural languages consist of these varying levels of structure. What the sentences of these different languages have in common is the deep structure, the underlying, formal, abstract structure.

To account for the way native speakers are able to "generate" the sentences of their language, the linguistic universals, Chomsky makes a distinction between competence and performance, a distinction which is crucial to understanding his theory. Linguistic competence has to do with ideal speakers and listeners who are completely unaffected by errors of any kind. They suffer from no outside distractions, no slips of the tongue, no memory lapses. Their competence relates to what they implicitly know about their language. Linguistic performance refers to how these ideal speakers actually use their language from day to day, how they actually produce sentences.

A linguistic theory then is a theory about an ideal speaker's competence. It is an idealization the way that any scientific theory is. It formulates its laws not as a description of actual behavior but in terms of abstract, underlying processes. Since many of the sentences produced by native speakers are ungrammatical, it would be difficult for the linguist to use these as the sole basis of his theorizing. Instead, he must abstract from the data the relevant features necessary for ascertaining the underlying principles.

A linguistic theory is mentalistic because it is as much concerned with underlying mental realities as it is with actual behavior. What is the complex mechanism that underlies linguistic competence? What are its constructs? How are they related to thought processes? Since the mind is not directly open to observation, the linguist must infer the characteristics of this underlying structure. The linguist then seeks empirical justification by determining how well a particular logical model explains the facts of communication, by observing the behavioral consequences, and by being able to predict future behavior.

Conceptual Theory of Discourse

As the above discussion indicates, this linguistic theory shares with scientific theories in general certain characteristics of form and outlook. The conceptual theory of discourse proposed in this study also shares some of the fundamental assumptions of these theories.

The conceptual theory of rhetoric is an explanatory theory of a much deeper sort than that of many rhetorics. The study of conceptual rhetoric is the study of the nature of human intellectual capacities. What are the innate organizing principles, the deeper underlying mental operations, the abstract mental structures that determine discourse? What hypotheses concerning this internalized system will account for the nature of its basic principles? Rhetorical patterns could not be produced in speech or in writing unless they were based on underlying mental processes. Although specific instances of discourse are concrete and individual, they do in fact reflect aspects of underlying, generalized processes. It is probable that innate properties of the human organism must be, at least in part, responsible for determining how we organize discourse. That is, the structural properties which underlie our mental operations must be genetically inherited. In generating discourse, the individual uses this underlying, abstract structure as a base. Then he supports this structure by filling in the details from the universe of discourse around him.

If the same innate structural patterns underlie all languages, then discourse patterns in different languages, regardless of surface differences, must be basically alike in many ways. We assume therefore that if we can discover common structural features of discourse in all languages that we can postulate the existence of discourse universals. So, for example, the rhetorician will expect discourse in all languages to exhibit the structural patterns of partition, classification, process, comparison, contrast, cause and effect, and so forth. In other words, all discourse seems to manifest, in written or spoken form, conceptual structures; the task of the rhetorician is to lay bare the underlying formal relations of these conceptual structures. But the constructs of the underlying patterns are abstract and ideal. How then can the rhetorician describe these structures?

A rhetorical description, like a linguistic description, is an idealization. Therefore, the rhetorician is not bound to describe patterns of discourse as they actually exist in speech or in writing. The rhetorician is free to abstract the ideal, underlying patterns from the empirical evidence, from the imperfections and irregularities of specific instances of discourse, and to classify these patterns as typical. So even if no actual pattern of discourse exhibits a particular structure precisely, in theory it would approximate it closely. Thus few essays reveal such patterns as classification, comparison, partition, analogy, or cause and effect in a "pure," formal arrangement. Usually, extended patterns of discourse consist of combinations of these and other patterns. Although traditional composition books and rhetoric books contain descriptions of these patterns, most provide weak descriptions, examples, and hints concerning conceptual processes, with no systematization in terms of underlying structures that cut across mixed patterns and with few or no generalizations to explain the types. Therefore, it is up to the rhetorician to abstract what he considers to be the basic, underlying structures.

The idea that a rhetorical description is an idealization leads to a complementary idea that a rhetorical description, like a linguistic description, must be an explication of an ideal speaker–writer's rhetorical competence rather than actual performance. Competence refers to what is implicitly known about the structure of discourse; performance refers to how discourse is actually produced.

One of the most important features of the conceptual theory of rhetoric, then, is that it seeks explanations for what is observed at some deeper level of reality. Another important characteristic of this theory is the importance it gives to wholes, to the logical priority of the whole over its parts. The whole and its parts can be explained satisfactorily only in terms of the particular relationships that exist among them. This viewpoint does not deny that the sentence and the paragraph have important structural characteristics of their own. But the sentence and the paragraph are more important as they relate to the complex network of relationships that link them to the longer discourse.

The theory of conceptual discourse may be characterized by the following propositions:

1. Thinking is structural.

2. Thinking often finds expression in patterns of symbols.

3. These patterns of symbols reveal structural characteristics.

4. When they appear in discourse, these structural characteristics manifest themselves as grammatical patterns and as conceptual patterns.

5. The conceptual patterns are implicit in the grammatical patterns. Sometimes these conceptual patterns transcend the grammatical patterns.

6. Conceptual patterns in discourse are symbolic manifestations of underlying thought processes.

7. Although the mind is inaccessible to observation, we can infer something about the underlying thought processes that produce discourse from observing and analyzing particular instances of discourse. Conversely, we can infer something about conceptual patterns of discourse from our knowledge of these underlying thought processes.

8. When patterns of thought manifest themselves as conceptual patterns of discourse, these conceptual patterns are embedded in sentences, in paragraphs, and in longer units of discourse. On the sentence level, they are stylistic. On the discourse level (the paragraph, the whole theme), they are organizational.

9. Because there is such a close relationship between certain conceptual patterns of discourse and certain thought processes, we infer that they share structural characteristics.

10. If thought processes and conceptual patterns of discourse display a close fit, and if, as some rhetoricians believe, the topics are symbolic manifestations of thought processes and reveal structural similarities to these thought processes, then it follows that there is a similarity of form between the topics and conceptual patterns of discourse. Therefore, conceptual patterns of discourse are topical and may accordingly serve a heuristic function.

11. But, as we have already pointed out, conceptual thought processes also manifest themselves on the sentence level. Therefore, conceptual patterns of sentences, conceptual patterns of extended discourse, and topical patterns of discovery are all structurally related. In other words, the topics of invention, the patterns of arrangement, and the stylistic aspects of sentences, when they reveal similar conceptual structures, are all closely interrelated. We

call these processes "topics" when they serve a heuristic function; we call them "patterns of arrangement" when they are used to organize discourse; we call them "stylistic" when they inform sentences. All, in fact, are symbolic manifestations of the same underlying thought processes.

That thinking is structural is a view which is being shared by more and more psychologists. We have already mentioned the theoretical approaches to thinking and perception as promulgated by gestalt psychologists such as Max Wertheimer, Kurt Koffka, and Wolfgang Kohler.[4] To these we might add the neurologically oriented theory of D. O. Hebb and the holistic theory of R. N. Sanford. Although these theories may not constitute "proof" for some critics, for rhetorical theory they do provide a reasonable basis for postulating the idea that thinking is structural. Further work by researchers in this field may confirm or refute this assumption. What many of these approaches have in common is the view that the organism impresses patterns on elements of experience and that it does so according to specific laws of development. To the gestaltist, field processes organize psychological energies during the thinking process and distribute them according to some kind of pattern. These patterns are characterized by simplicity, closure, regularity, and symmetry. It is interesting to note that these terms have their rhetorical counterparts in such familiar compositional terms as unity, coherence, rhythm, and balance. To the neurologically oriented theorist, cell assemblies organize phase sequences or patterns on the basis of past experience. This approach differs from that of gestalt psychology by suggesting that the patterns produced during the thinking process are learned slowly and by repeated experiences.

The idea that thinking often finds expression in patterns of symbols can be verified by common sense. However, thinking does not always manifest itself in symbols. For example, thinking takes place in the act of perception. A person can observe on the perceptual level that one tree is larger than another tree, or that it is greener or shaped differently. This kind of thinking does not require verbal symbols. Also many kinds of operational activities involved in solving problems do not require symbols. However, when a symbol is present, we can always infer that some kind of thinking activity has taken place. Music, poetry, painting, dancing, plays, dreams, rituals are all symbolic patterns that mirror the structure of thought. Our primary concern in rhetoric, of course, is to determine how the structure of thought is expressed in patterns of discourse.

Patterns of symbols do reveal structural characteristics. The proof of this statement is implicit in its formulation. Patterns do not exist without patterning. But aside from this seeming tautology, we have ample proof in the arts and in the sciences. The geometrical proportions of the paintings of Renaissance artists, the "concrete" paintings of Hans Arp and Max Bill, the structural paintings of the cubists, the topological forms of modern sculpture, even the nonfigurative art of such painters as Jackson Pollock reveal structural characteristics. Chemical and mathematical equations, the model of the DNA molecule, the axioms of geometry, the propositions of a syllogism, the elements in a plot, the repetition of a theme in music, a succession of images, the structure of a sonnet, the rhythm of verse—all reveal structural characteristics.

When these patterns of symbols appear in discourse, they manifest themselves as grammatical patterns and as conceptual patterns. The conceptual patterns are implicit in the grammatical patterns. Sometimes the conceptual patterns transcend the grammatical patterns. On the sentence level, the work of the structural linguists and of the transformational grammarians has amply illustrated the importance of structure in grammar. Immediate constituent analysis reveals the binary quality of grammatical constructions. Transformational analysis reveals deeper levels of structure and form than are apparent on the surface level. Beyond the sentence, the analyses of paragraphs by Francis Christensen illustrate the fundamental grammatical principles of coordination and subordination in the structure of discourse.

Conceptual patterns abound on almost every level of discourse: the sentence, the paragraph, and the essay. Some typical examples of these patterns are: comparison, contrast, division into parts, enumeration, narration, description, exemplification, syllogistic progression, analogy, metaphor, repetition, and the like. We call these patterns "conceptual" because the words which constitute these patterns symbolize concepts and when these words occur in interlocking groups or constructs, we may rightly call these constructs "conceptual patterns." That these conceptual patterns are implicit in the grammatical patterns should be obvious. For example, in the sentence, "A tulip is shaped like a bell," the grammatical pattern is that of a simple sentence with a noun phrase subject ("a tulip"), a verb ("is shaped"), and a prepositional phrase ("like a bell"). But the conceptual pattern is that of a comparison: A tulip— is shaped like— a bell (or in more abstract terms, $A \sim B$). Embedded in the grammatical pattern is the conceptual pattern. When we are dealing with larger patterns of discourse, we cannot always show a one to one relationship between a grammatical pattern and a conceptual pattern. If, for example, the underlying conceptual pattern of a complete essay is that of a comparison, quite obviously some of the sentences and some of the paragraphs will not directly reflect the conceptual pattern. Some sentences and some paragraphs may be introductory, some may be transitional, and some may be concluding. Or it may be that a sequence of sentences or parts of sentences will carry the burden of comparison. Or it may be that alternate sentences carry the intent of the comparison whereas others may qualify, modify, or even digress from the comparison. Yet it is possible to abstract the underlying conceptual scheme from and in spite of the irregularities of the grammatical pattern.

Perhaps at this point, because the terms "concept" and "conceptual structure" have been used with such frequency, we ought to clarify these terms even further. Contrary to the popular view, a concept is not a word, a sound, or an image, although I see no reason to refrain from calling a word a verbal concept just as long as we realize that a word is actually a symbolic representation of a concept or of the mental process of conceptualizing. What a concept is might partially be explained by comparing it to a phoneme in the field of linguistics. A phoneme is not actually a speech sound; a phoneme is an abstraction, a unit of the phonological system. People make speech sounds, and each of these sounds is infinitely varied. Thus the phoneme /k/ is not a speech sound in itself, but a symbol which represents a variety of similar sounds articulated differently by different people. Similarly, an image or a word is not a concept. A concept is an abstraction, a unit of thinking behavior.[5] Sometimes a concept is verbalized by the thinking individual; sometimes it is not. Conceptualizing refers to certain kinds of intellectual operations. Since a concept is really an abstract unit of thinking behavior, it is difficult to distinguish it from thinking itself. A symbol such as a word is distinct from thinking. It is a product of thinking. A concept, then, has no objective reality. It is identical with the process of conceptualizing. When we give names to such processes, these verbal labels symbolize the mental processes. Thus classifying, serializing, analyzing, comparing, and defining are verbal labels which are typical examples of conceptualizing. Words are important, however, because they represent and mediate concepts.

If words represent and mediate concepts, how is this done? Some words, the so-called "content words" of our language such as nouns, verbs, adjectives, and adverbs symbolize people, objects, events, processes, qualities, and operations. Words such as articles, prepositions, and conjunctions identify the relationships that exist among the content words. In the absence of the immediate stimuli which are the objects of sense experience, we can use words to represent and mediate these stimuli as well as the resulting concepts. Thus if I use the word *dog* in a sentence, the symbol derives from the total concept of what in my experience I have found a dog to be. This concept includes memory traces of my original perceptions, verbal labels, affective responses, intensional and extensional meanings, associated concepts, and so forth. The "meaning" of the concept resides in my experiences of all dogs, together with all of their attributes. And every time I experience different dogs, my original concept will change. But the word is not the concept. The concept is in me. It is part of my thinking activity. When I put the word *dog* in a sentence, I connect it with other words which symbolize concepts or relationships among concepts. This connected string of concepts then becomes a construct. Corresponding then to the grammatical pattern of which the word *dog* is a part is an actual pattern of concepts, a construct, which is part of my mental activity. Conceptualizing consists in manipulating these concepts and manifests itself in such varied mental activities as identifying, abstracting, analyzing, comparing, and the like.[6]

Thus when I use the term *concept,* I may use it to refer to actual mental activity, to an abstract unit of thinking activity, or to a word which represents that unit. And when I use the term *conceptual structure,* I may use it to denote a group of interlocking concepts or to its symbolic manifestation in a verbal pattern.

One of the difficulties in using the term *conceptual* in rhetorical theory is that the topics of invention, the patterns of arrangement, and the aspects of style that I refer to as "conceptual" are often referred to as "rhetorical" by other writers. And clearly there is some overlapping. But I would like to use the word *rhetorical* in a more restricted sense and the word *conceptual* in a broader and more inclusive sense. Thus, for example, I would consider the topics of classification and comparison as "conceptual" topics because they can be related to perceptual and conceptual activities in the thinking process, even in the absence of language. On the other hand, I would consider the topics of possible and impossible and of past and future fact as "rhetorical" topics. These play little part in my scheme except insofar as they can be subsumed under the more general categories of contradictories or contraries. Similarly, I would consider classification and comparison as "conceptual" patterns of arrangement on the paragraph level or on the discourse level, but the patterns of problem and solution or question and answer I consider to be "rhetorical" patterns. Finally, I use the term "conceptual," as it relates to style, to refer to such schemes and tropes as antithesis and metaphor. But I use the word "rhetorical" to refer to stylistic categories such as loose, periodic, and balanced. Hopefully, the meaning of the term "conceptual" should become even more apparent in the process of further delineating this theory.

If words are symbols of concepts, and if organized groups of words are symbols of conceptual structures, and if conceptual structures are a part of the mental processes, then conceptual patterns in discourse are symbolic manifestations of underlying thought processes. As we have just pointed out, words are symbols of concepts, organized groups of words are symbols of conceptual structures, and conceptual structures are a part of the mental processes. Therefore, the conclusion follows logically. Objective behavior always permits inference to thinking processes. Thus, if someone says to me, "I hear a bird singing," I can infer that perceptual thinking has taken place. If I observe someone working out the solution to a problem, I can infer that operational thinking has taken place. And if I observe a religious ritual, I can infer that symbolic activity has taken place.

Although the mind is inaccessible to observation, we can infer something about the underlying thought processes that produce discourse from observing and analyzing particular instances of discourse. Conversely, we can infer something about conceptual patterns of discourse from our knowledge of these underlying thought processes. This argument may appear to be circular, but it is not necessarily so. Suppose we postulate a rhetorical model which depicts the structure of certain underlying thought processes in a certain manner. If the constructs of this model explain the facts of rhetorical communication and if these facts of rhetorical communication can be shown to be behavioral consequences of this model, then we can infer something about conceptual structures of discourse from our knowledge of the structure of this model which represents these underlying thought processes. Or we can proceed from our observations and analyses of particular instances of discourse. If we can adequately describe conceptual patterns of discourse, we can then abstract certain features and infer from them something about corresponding thought processes. For example, suppose that we postulate as part of our conceptual model of underlying thought processes two categories, classification and comparison. Now there is already ample evidence from psychological literature to confirm that classifying and comparing are basic mental processes. But whether or not this were so, we would be justified in considering the behavioral consequences of these categories (people do classify and compare) and in seeking empirical justification for these categories in particular instances of discourse. Are there in fact sentences, paragraphs, and extended units of discourse which depict these processes? Suppose, on the other hand, we examine mature instances of discourse and we identify certain patterns that correspond to conceptual thought processes. Then we can infer from these patterns something about the underlying thought processes that produced these patterns.

When patterns of thought manifest themselves as conceptual patterns in discourse, these conceptual patterns are embedded in sentences, in paragraphs, and in longer units of discourse. On the sentence level, they are stylistic. On the discourse level (the paragraph, the whole theme), they are organizational. We have hypothesized that patterns of thought do manifest themselves as conceptual patterns in discourse and that these conceptual patterns are embedded in sentences, in paragraphs, and in longer units of discourse. The following patterns can be found on almost every level of discourse: description, narration, classification, comparison, contrast, analogy, cause and effect, partition, and enumeration. When they are embedded in sentences, we call them aspects of style. When they are embedded in paragraphs and extended units of discourse, we call them aspects of structure. We do these things, of course, by definition. There is no reason, for example, why we cannot call features of an extended metaphor stylistic. Yet, for purposes of analysis, we point to metaphorical features on the sentence level and call them stylistic. When they are repeated in subsequent sentences, we call them features of structure or organizational patterns.

Because there is such a close relationship between certain conceptual patterns of discourse and certain thought processes, we infer that they share structural characteristics. For example, if I compare the shape of a tulip to the shape of a bell, in the act of conceptualizing this relationship I must bring them together in my mind. Among the many laws of association involved in my conceptualizing this relationship are those of abstraction, contiguity, and similarity. No matter how I try to conceptualize this relationship, I must bring the concepts of tulip and bell together in some kind of contiguous correspondence. On the perceptual level, I may actually observe a tulip and a bell together. On a more abstract level, I can bring them together in my imagination. Or I can substitute symbols in the form of words. Even then, I must somehow bring these words together on the printed page. Thus my conceptual thought processes and my conceptual sentence pattern share the structural characteristics of contiguity and similarity.

If thought processes and conceptual patterns of discourse display a close fit, and if, as some rhetoricians believe, the topics are symbolic manifestations of thought processes and reveal structural similarities to these thought processes, then it follows that there is a similarity of form between the topics and conceptual patterns of discourse. Therefore, conceptual patterns of discourse are topical and may accordingly serve a heuristic function. To illustrate this argument, let us consider three basic processes of the mind: analyzing (or dividing into parts), classifying, and comparing. We consider these to be fundamental mental processes. Analogous to these mental processes are their symbolic manifestations in discourse which take the form of conceptual patterns of discourse. In other words, there are paragraph patterns and extended patterns of discourse which we label "division into parts," "classification," and "comparison." But these mental processes can also be thought of as "topics" and can accordingly be used to probe a particular subject in order to find out more about it. Therefore, analysis, classification, and comparison can be considered from different points of view as being mental processes, or topics, or patterns of organization. Conceptual patterns of discourse are in fact inseparable from their topical counterparts and thus may serve a heuristic function.

But as we have already pointed out, conceptual thought processes also manifest themselves on the sentence level. Therefore conceptual patterns of sentences, conceptual patterns of extended discourse, and topical patterns of discovery are all structurally related. In other words, the topics of invention, the patterns of arrangement, and the stylistic aspects of sentences, when they reveal similar conceptual structures, are all closely interrelated. We call these processes "topics" when they serve a heuristic function; we call them "patterns of arrangement" when they are used to organize discourse; we call them "stylistic" when they inform sentences. All, in fact, are symbolic manifestations of the same underlying thought processes. To use our familiar examples, analysis, classification, and comparison may be considered, depending on our point of view, mental processes, topics, patterns of organization, or techniques of style.

This aspect of rhetorical theory is a dramatic departure from more traditional points of view which conceive of the separate parts of rhetoric as being distinct and compartmentalized. Thus, in classical rhetoric, the topics are distinct from the formal pattern of arrangement, and style is distinct from both. Even in more recent approaches to rhetorical theory, as in the tagmemic theory of Young, Becker, and Pike, the heuristic probe is something quite different from the patterns of arrangement into which one puts the results of the probe. And style, as in classical rhetoric, is something that has to do with sentences. Very few rhetoricians have hinted at the idea that patterns of discourse or figures of style might serve a heuristic function.[7] No one, as far as I have been able to determine, has ever pointed out the complex interrelationships that exist among the processes of invention, arrangement, style, and thinking.

Thus far we have considered the conceptual theory of rhetoric in terms of a semiformal deductive system of conditional propositions. Quite often, however, a theoretical system may be better elucidated if it is put into the form of a picture or model which somehow reflects the inner structure of the reality to be described. Such a model may be mimetic, diagrammatic, classificatory, and so on. The following chapters will depict the conceptual theory of rhetoric in diagrammatic form, while at the same time relating its principle postulates to the traditional divisions of rhetoric into invention (and memory), arrangement, and style.

Notes

1. Stephen C. Pepper, *World Hypotheses* (Berkeley: University of California Press, 1970), p. 91.

2. See, for example, the following references: R. B. Braithwaite, "Models in the Empirical Sciences," in *Readings in the Philosophy of Science,* ed. Baruch A. Brody (Englewood Cliffs, N.J.: Prentice-Hall, Inc., 1970), p. 268; N. R. Campbell, "What Is a Theory?" in *Readings in the Philosophy of Science,* ed. Baruch A. Brody (Englewood Cliffs, N.J.: Prentice-Hall, 1970), p. 252; Rom Harre, *The Principles of Scientific Thinking* (Chicago: The University of Chicago Press, 1970), p. 14; Ernest

Nagel, *The Structure of Science* (New York: Harcourt Brace Jovanovich, Inc., 1961), pp. 21, 90.

3. The following discussion is derived primarily from these sources: Noam Chomsky, *Aspects of the Theory of Syntax* (Cambridge, Mass.: The M.I.T. Press, 1965), pp. 3–9, 18–30; Jerrold J. Katz, *The Philosophy of Language* (New York: Harper & Row, 1966), pp. 107–118, 176–183; John Lyons, *Noam Chomsky* (New York: Harper & Row, 1970), pp. 37–47, 107–121.

4. J. J. Gibson, *The Senses Considered as Perceptual Systems* (Boston: Houghton Mifflin Co., 1966); D. O. Hebb, *Organization of Behavior: A Neuro-psychological Theory* (New York: John Wiley and Sons, Inc., 1949); Kurt Koffka, *Principles of Gestalt Psychology* (New York: Liveright Publishing Corp., 1935); Wolfgang Kohler, *Gestalt Psychology* (New York: Liveright Publishing Corp., 1947); Max Wertheimer, *Productive Thinking,* Enlarged Edition, ed. Michael Wertheimer (New York: Harper & Brothers Publishers, 1959).

5. The primary source for this view is: Hans G. Furth, *Thinking Without Language* (New York: The Free Press, 1966), pp. 19–23, 190–197, 224–228. This view can also be found in the works of Vygotsky and Piaget.

6. This discussion derives in part from the following source: Raymond G. Smith, *Speech-Communication: Theory and Models* (New York: Harper & Row, 1970), pp. 7–9, 44, 73–77.

7. As Sister Miriam Joseph points out, however, the figurists (Sherry, Peacham, Puttenham) during the Renaissance included in their treatises as figures many examples that we would consider illustrative of the topics of invention. Sister Miriam Joseph, C.S.C., *Shakespeare's Use of the Arts of Language* (New York: Columbia University Press, 1947), pp. 17, 36, 37.

IV

INVENTION AND MEMORY

The Topics and the Commonplaces

Any systematic treatment of invention must begin with the related concepts of the topics, the commonplaces, and the art of memory in classical rhetoric. The word *topic* is derived from the Greek word *topos,* meaning "a place." This word in turn is derived from the Greek word *topikos,* meaning "of a place" or "commonplace." The Latin word *topica* is derived from the Greek word *topikos* or *topika.* The word *commonplace* is a translation of the Latin *locus communis* which is itself a translation of the Greek *koinos topos.* Thus the *commonplaces* of Renaissance England, the *loci* of Rome, and the *topoi* of Greece are rough etymological equivalents.

Although it is relatively easy to trace the origin of these words, it is much more difficult to determine their exact meanings as they were used by classical rhetoricians and by later scholars who followed in the classical tradition. Despite this difficulty, however, it is possible to trace two main lines of development. The first line interprets the topics as being content-laden, to be used as subject matter or as prefabricated arguments that could be directly inserted into a discourse. The second line of development views the topics as abstract and analytical, to be used to probe any subject whatever.[1]

The first line of development seems to have originated with Cicero and Quintilian and was followed by Medieval and Renaissance scholars. In this view, the topics consisted of stock arguments, snippets of oratorical material, praises or dispraises of people and things, brief treatises on virtues and vices, thematic material, exempla, proverbs, sententiae, quotations, and the like, which could be inserted into longer orations or which could be used as arguments in themselves. For example, sententiae such as *Fortuna est caeca, Philosophia est art vitae,* and *Modum tenere debem* could be used as arguments in giving moral advice or as premises in an argument. They could also be used as theses to be amplified and developed in a brief discourse. Another example is the use of stock arguments to be inserted almost verbatim into a discourse. Typical of these were the cosmological arguments for proving the existence of God, which can be traced back to Thomas Aquinas who systematized them in the thirteenth century. These arguments were frequently cast in syllogistic form. Most frequent are the arguments from cause and effect, from the orderly design of the universe, from the degrees of natural perfection, and from the contingent nature of things in the universe. This view of the topics is by no means dead. It still exists in the teaching of Latin and scholastic philosophy in some schools and universities. Perhaps a direct line of development can even be traced to the much maligned freshman composition readers in our own day which seem to bear some resemblance to at least one kind of commonplace book which listed its topics under subject matter headings or thematic headings.

The second line of development, which views the topics as analytical, seems to have its origin in the works of Aristotle and Cicero, with subsequent developments in the treatises of John of Garland, the dialectical places of Leonard Cox and M. Blunderville, and the dialectical system of Peter Ramus. Most of us are already familiar with the common topics of Aristotle in the *Rhetoric,* which were extended by Cicero in the *Topica.* They included definition, partition, comparison, analogy, antecedent, consequence, cause, effect, genus, species and the like. These topics may be considered analytical although some scholars would prefer to reserve that designation for the logical categories of Aristotle in the *Organon.* Some typical examples are substance, quality, relation, time, and space. The topics of John of Garland, who composed an important literary manual for instruction in the *ars poetica* in the thirteenth century, follow the line of development set forth by Aristotle and Cicero. The reader must remember that rhetoric and poetics were not yet considered separate disciplines so that John of Garland's topics for inventing in the poetic arts are really analytical topics. They consisted of the following categories: *ubi, quid, quale, ad quid,* and *qualiter.* The topic of *qualiter* was further divided into such subtopics as definition, exposition, repetition, and metonomy. The topical categories of journalism (who, what, when, where, why) are closely related to John of Garland's topics. The dialectical places of the Renaissance, as exemplified in England by *The Art or Crafte of Rhetoryke* of Leonard Cox and *The Arte of Logicke* of M. Blunderville, also follow in the tradition of the analytical topics. The logical categories of Cox included definition, causes, parts, effects, similarities, and contraries. Some of these topics were to be used in analyzing simple terms and ideas; others were to be used in analyzing compound terms. The "artificial places" or topics of Blunderville embraced such topics as definition, description, interpretation, the whole and its parts, signs, circumstances, cause, effect, contraries, and contradictories. The dialectical system of Peter Ramus in France was also a system of analytical topics. It consisted of arranging a subject in dialectical order by dividing it into parts and then following its movement from the general to the specific. More recent examples of the analytical topics are the categories of Immanuel Kant and the tabular categories of Peter Roget in the *Thesaurus.* The approach to invention as set forth in this study follows the line of development which views the topics as analytical.

Memory

The art of memory was the technique by which an orator was able to memorize long speeches for delivery. Yet the art of memory is as inextricably bound up with the art of invention and the art of reasoning as it is with delivery. Aristotle's idea that the mind thinks in images seems to be the most direct source of this connection. If the mind thinks in images, then what better mnemonic devices are there than images? Thus, according to Cicero and Quintilian, if we wish to remember persons or ideas we should choose images that are strong and sharp or striking and unusual, and associate them with the persons or ideas to be remembered. Then we should place the images in a certain order. In this way the images, and consequently the persons or ideas to be remembered, will be more easily recalled. It is not always clear where exactly these images are to be placed. Those rhetoricians who would relate the art of memory to Aristotle's theory of knowledge would place them in the mind. Other rhetoricians would contend that the "places" in which images are supposed to be stored are nothing more than spatial metaphors. Cicero, for example, or the author of *Ad Herennium,* uses the metaphor of a house to depict the places where images are stored. At other times he uses an arch or columns, or some kind of architectural space. Quintilian also uses the metaphor of a house or large building. He would have an orator place images, corresponding to the parts of a speech to be remembered, in the rooms of a building in a certain order. Then the orator, in attempting to remember the speech, would move from room to room, retrieving the points in the speech in the designated order. Renaissance scholars conceived of the memory places as being in the mind as well as in more concrete locations such as in notebooks and commonplace books. Other scholars, those who viewed the topics as analytical, conceived of the memory places as more abstract. There are hints of this view in Plato. Instead of the Aristotelian concept of the mind thinking in mental images, in Plato's works we get the idea of the mind already equipped with abstract forms and innate categories. In Plato's view, memory consists of recollecting these abstract forms and archetypal ideas. Quintilian's concept of the memory places is more concrete than Plato's, but at times he gives hints of being dissatisfied with the classical view. Fitting ideas and words to images and then depositing them in storage places, Quintilian maintained, imposes a double burden on the memory, for we would need to have an almost infinite number of images in order to recall even a short oration. He suggested that the memorizer either learn the speech by heart or commit it to writing and then use these abstract "memory tracks" as a guide in remembering. Raymond Lull's system of memory (1272) relates more directly than any previous system to the analytical topics, and works directly with the abstractions of the Aristotelian categories. To Lull, memory was the art of investigation, and the categories were a means of pursuing that investigation. Because these categories were so abstract, Lull used visual aids such as diagrams, schematizations, and figures of various sorts as helps in remembering these categories. Peter Ramus (1515–72), the French dialectician, arranged his categories in dialectical order for ease of memory. This abstract order in itself then becomes the stimulus for the memory.

The conceptual theory of rhetoric follows the line of development which views the topics as abstract and analytical. It conceives of the topics as symbols of abstract, underlying mental processes which take place in the brain. In other words, these topics have a psychological reality. But since the brain is inaccessible to observation, we can only infer the characteristics of these underlying processes. We do this by constructing a model which depicts the structure of the components. If the behavioral consequences match the logical constructs of the model, then we are justified in accepting the model as a significant hypothesis. In setting up a model to depict certain aspects of these mental processes, not just any data will do; we need to abstract and to categorize only those constructs which represent mental processes that seem relevant to the study of rhetoric. Obviously, some categories will be more useful than others in helping us to identify relevant aspects of the system. The categories of this logical model define implicitly the basic constructs of the system.

The following series of models in the form of branching tree diagrams attempt to depict the characteristics of some abstract, underlying mental processes. The categories of these models also provide a heuristic procedure which should be useful in exploring any subject and in generating new insights and ideas.

Figure 1

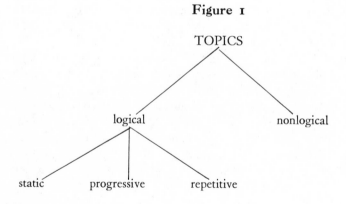

The first diagram (Figure 1) depicts the two main divisions of the topics, the logical and the nonlogical. The logical topics are divided into three subcategories: static, progressive, and repetitive, categories suggested by Kenneth Burke's discussion of form in *Counter-Statement*. (These categories can be viewed as "forming" as well as "informed," that is, they can serve a heuristic function.) The static logical topics are then broken down as indicated in Figure 2.

Figure 2

STATIC LOGICAL TOPICS

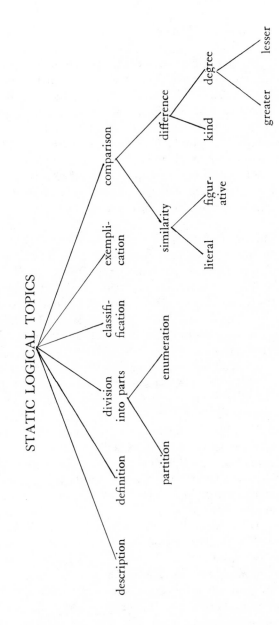

Static Logical Topics

The superordinate node dominates the static logical topics. All other categories are subsumed under it, and it is divided into six main categories: description (What is it? What are its constituent parts? How is it organized in space?); definition (What are its limits or boundaries? What is its genus? What is its species?); division into parts, with its subcategories of partition (What are its pieces, parts, or sections? How may they logically be divided?); and enumeration (What is the logical order? What is the exact number?); classification (What are its common attributes? What are its basic categories?); exemplification (What are some representative instances, examples, or illustrations?), and comparison.

The topic of comparison is divided into two subtopics, similarity and difference. Similarity deals with resemblances, difference with dissimilarities. The topic of similarity (What is it like?) is subdivided into the categories of literal similarity (similarity in kind) and figurative similarity (similarity in relationship). The topic of difference (What is the condition or degree of dissimilarity?) is divided into difference in kind and difference in degree. Difference in degree breaks down into greater (more, better) or lesser (less, worse).

In addition to the hierarchial relationships of the categories, a horizontal reading of the categories reveals relationships that transcend particular categories; description, for example, is related to definition. Describing something provides a means of analyzing and identifying it. Defining is a kind of abstract description. Definition, division into parts, and classification share fundamental relationships: to define is to limit or set boundaries to a thing by separating it from other things (division); to define is to put the thing to be defined into a class (classification); to classify is to divide into categories, so classification and division are related categories. Exemplification is related to definition (giving examples is one way of defining), to division in parts (examples are parts of wholes), and to classification (each example is a member of a group or class of persons and things).

On the other side of the diagram, the topic of literal similarity contrasts with that of figurative similarity in that literal similarity is concerned with things in the same order of being whereas figurative similarity is concerned with things in a different order of being. The topic of literal similarity is related to that of difference in kind: both are concerned with classes or types of things in the same order of being. The relationship between difference in kind and difference in degree should be apparent.

Further relationships exist between the topic of comparison and the other superordinate categories. For example, classification is based on grouping similar things; division into parts is based on differences. Thus there is a relationship between the topic of classification and the topic of similarity and between the topic of division into parts and that of difference. Definition differentiates; therefore, this topic relates to the topic of difference.

The third diagram (Figure 3) depicts the main divisions of the progressive logical topics. These consist of narration, process, cause and effect, and syllogistic progression.

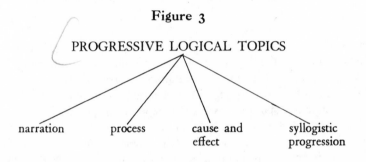

Figure 3

PROGRESSIVE LOGICAL TOPICS

narration   process   cause and   syllogistic
                                    effect   progression

Narration (What happened? When did it happen?) is related to process (How did it happen? How does it work?); to cause and effect (Why did it happen? What caused or produced it? What are the results or consequences?); and to syllogistic progression (If certain things happen, then what must follow?). A horizontal relating of the progressive logical topics to the static logical topics reveals the following relationships. Narration is related to enumeration (a narrative is a recounting in time), to exemplification (examples can be *exempla*), and to process (a narration, like a process, is a succession of actions). Process is related to narration (as indicated above), to enumeration (a process is a sequence of steps or events), and to cause and effect (the steps in a process are usually causally related). Finally, cause and effect, in addition to being related to process, is also related to enumeration (causes may develop in a series), to narration (cause and effect relationships are essential to plots), and to syllogistic progression (syllogistic reasoning advances step by step, in a causally developed sequence).

The repetitive logical topics are graphically depicted in diagram four (Figure 4) as follows:

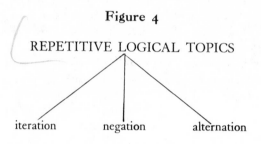

Figure 4

REPETITIVE LOGICAL TOPICS

iteration   negation   alternation

Iteration is the repeated statement of an idea again and again under new guises. It may be the repetition of the same idea for emphasis or it may be a restatement of the same idea in another form for clarity or precision. Negation can be a form of repetition. Alternation is the process of moving between iteration (positive assertion or repetition) and negation (negative assertion or repetition). Principles of repetition are more often related to form than to invention, but rephrasing, restating, and summarizing can be useful forms of invention. The repetitive topics are clearly related to such topics as enumeration (repeating a number of things in an orderly sequence), exemplification (examples are repeated in inductive arguments), and narration and process (both involve the repetition of actions). These are just a few of the many interrelationships that exist among all the topics.

The topics, then, can best be described as categories which reflect thought processes. The world we perceive includes not only objects and events located in space and time, but also the relationships that bind these objects and events to each other and to the perceiver. These conceptual categories therefore are *relational* conceptual categories.

As the foregoing discussion indicates, the advantages of putting the categories into some kind of graphic scheme, such as a branching tree diagram, are many. Such a diagram lays bare the conceptual scheme so that the reader can take it in at a glance. The model also isolates and identifies the individual categories and suggests ways in which they can be related. Ideally, we might some day be able to depict more significant relationships, to illustrate, for example, that certain categories are possibly transformations of more basic underlying processes. In the meantime, however, our conceptual model will have to be roughly classificatory and tentative. As we add new categories we will certainly have to alter the basic relationships.

Another advantage of the model is that it lends itself to easy memorization, since categories such as comparison, contrast, and metaphor tend to cluster in logical units. The idea, of course, is to get the individual to internalize these topics (and the questions which they suggest) so that they can be used for subsequent invention. It might be argued that the mental processes which these categories represent are already internalized so that this process is essentially wasteful. The answer, is, of course, that we want to make the process of invention more self-conscious and more economical for compositional purposes. A scheme such as the one I propose is one kind of possibility for this purpose.

Nonlogical Topics

Rhetoric, for the most part, has concerned itself primarily with logical thought processes related to problem solving. But psychological studies of autistic behavior, research on psychedelic drugs, studies in creativity, and in Freudian dream theory all suggest that nonlogical mental processes play a major role in thinking. In addition, recent neurological research on "split-brain" patients has revealed that human beings have two modes of consciousness (perhaps roughly akin to our two kinds of topics, the logical and the nonlogical) and that these two modes of consciousness are not merely metaphors, but have a physiological basis.

Situated dead center in the middle of the brain is the largest and most mysterious information transmission system in the world—the corpus callosum. With it intact, the two halves of the body have no secrets from one another. With it sectioned, the two halves become two different conscious mental spheres, each with its own experienced base and control system for behavioral operations. Just as conjoined twins are two different people sharing a common body, the callosum-sectioned human has two separate conscious

spheres sharing a common brain stem, head, and body. . . . The
natural organization of the mammalian brain is such that a slice
of the surgeon's knife through the midline commissures produces
two separate, but equal, cognitive systems each with its own
abilities to learn, emote, think, and act.[2]

The idea that the mind has two modes of consciousness has been around
for a very long time. It manifests itself in such familiar dichotomies as
reason versus the imagination, logic versus intuition, deliberation versus
inspiration, the rational and the irrational, the real and the ideal, classicism
and romanticism, science and art, the conscious mind and the subconscious mind. For years, some psychologists have reminded us that the
Freudian categories of the mind were to be taken merely as useful
metaphors. Now it appears that there is experimental evidence to prove,
at least in part, that these categories may have a localized existence in
the brain.[3]

The brain is divided into two main parts or hemispheres, which
are joined by the corpus callosum, a large band of interconnecting com-
missural fibers. Each hemisphere is apparently highly specialized and
each has unique functions. The left hemisphere processes information
analytically and sequentially; it is responsible for language, logic, linear
thought, and rationality. The right hemisphere processes information
more diffusely; it is responsible for imaginative thinking, intuition, spatial
orientation, bodily awareness, and creativity. Despite these specialized
activities, the processes of these two hemispheres are not mutually exclusive. Some language activities go on in the right hemisphere, and both
hemispheres can at times function either simultaneously or independ-
ently. In normal persons the two kinds of thought interact so that often
we seem to be operating in both modes at the same time.[4] Rhetorical
invention must incorporate both modes.

The following diagram (Figure 5) is an exploratory attempt to
delineate a few of the so-called nonlogical topics. Imagining is the process
of forming mental images, concepts, or word pictures that are not actually
present to the senses. Of the nonlogical topics, imagining seems to be the
most fundamental, and it overlaps with the others. Imagining includes
the evocation of visual, auditory, kinesthetic, tactile, gustatory, and olfactory images. Although the primary function of the imagination is that of
evoking and creating images, it also operates on the level of feeling, think-

Figure 5

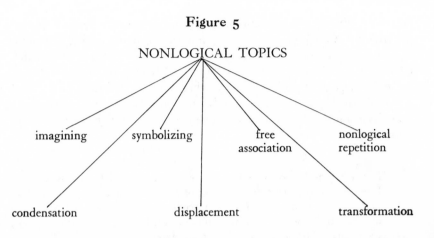

NONLOGICAL TOPICS

imagining   symbolizing   free
                            association   nonlogical
                                          repetition

condensation   displacement   transformation

ing, sensation, and intuition. The imagination can be reproductive (the recalling of images) or it can be productive and heuristic, combining and recombining elements in a new way.

Symbolizing is the process of representing abstract ideas by means of analogy. A symbol is a condensation of two or more images, words, concepts, or ideas into a single element. Symbolizing is closely related to imagining because the symbol must be visualized before it can be used. Some psychologists believe that there is such a close relationship between the conscious and unconscious processes that conscious visualization of symbols can be used to set unconscious mental processes in motion. Thus symbols mediate between conscious and unconscious psychological processes. Since symbolizing is based on analogy and since analogy is a useful heuristic process, then symbolizing can be used as a heuristic technique for perceiving new relationships.

Free association is the process of linking an image, a word, or an idea to some other image, word, or idea. It is a spontaneous, unconstrained association of ideas, feelings, and emotions. Some psychologists consider this process to be logical, but others contend that the linking of images and ideas is more often than not based on chance associations. Like symbolizing, free association is related to imagining, since the images and words must first be evoked before they can be associated. Free association has already been used with moderate success in the classroom by teachers as a heuristic procedure for invention.

Logical repetition has its counterpart in the nonlogical processes of the mind. Like logical repetition, nonlogical repetition is the repeated presentation of a word, an image, or an idea. It is unlike logical repetition in that the connections between elements seem to be based on accidental, haphazard, or chance associations. Some kinds of pathological thinking use nonlogical repetition to produce what some psychologists have called a "word salad," a cluster of words and phrases loosely connected by superficial associations and characterized by private symbols and private meanings:

> I am the President of the United States. I will be the last President. I will not be present because I am not a resident of Pennsylvania. Pennsylvania in Transylvania. Transcontinental trains are the best kind. In trains when it rains. Rains in April bring May flowers. Flour makes bread. Cast your bread upon the water. Blood is thicker than water. I am of royal blood. Red blood, black blood, black power. I am the most powerful except for policemen and police dogs. The German shepherd was the best dog this year.[5]

The kinds of repetition involved are varied. There is identical word repetition: President, Pennsylvania, rains, bread, blood, black, dog. There are words derived from the same root or words similar in sound, apparently based on the same root, but actually based on false etymology: President/present/resident; Pennsylvania/Transylvania/transcontinental. And there are rhyming words: president/resident; trains/rains; and words that are homophones: flower/flour. Ordinary thinking uses similar techniques, but the repetition is not as disjointed or random.

Condensation is the process by which images and ideas are combined in a single element; symbolization is one kind of condensation. In condensation, the images and ideas contain both manifest and latent content. This is especially apparent in dreams when an image of a person may appear with the characteristics of several different people. In language, condensation takes the form of puns and contradictory meanings (for example, *taboo* means "holy" as well as "unclean"). Condensation is related to bipolar thinking, and is generally considered to be prelogical, undirected, and undifferentiated. The Tagitu, an ancient Chinese symbol, is a good example of the kinds of forms involved in bipolar thinking. It combines images and ideas such as "light and dark," "right and left," and "masculine and feminine" into one concept. Neologisms (i.e., new word formations: *slithy,* from "lithe" and "slimy") are yet another form of condensation.[6]

Displacement is the process whereby an image or idea is replaced by another image or idea. Displacement appears in language in the form of allusions and euphemisms. It is also an important aspect of dream distortion.

Transformation is the process of changing the shape, form, or appearance of an image or concept without altering its semantic value, and it, too, often appears in dreams, where it takes the form of images that are transmuted from one shape to another. Thus the image of a tree in a dream, symbolizing inexhaustible life, growth, regeneration, and immortality, may be transformed into a ladder, the Cross of Redemption, or a mountain.

The nonlogical topics are related to various mental states such as fantasy, hallucination, dreams, reverie, creative thinking, and meditation. Fantasy is the process of forming images or concepts of things that are not actually present to the senses. The images that are formed are often disordered, bizarre in form, fanciful, exotic, strange, or visionary. This more or less connected series of images usually satisfies some wish or desire. Hallucination may be considered a kind of autistic thinking in which sights, sounds, and smells are apparently perceived even though they may not be actually present. The associative processes involved in such thinking often result in disjointed, random associations. Dreaming may be considered a form of nonlogical thinking which frees the dreamer from the limitations of conscious thought. Dreams consist of a sequence of sensations, images, and thoughts which pass through the mind during sleep. A dream is a symbolic event which, according to Freud, represents a wish fulfillment. A reverie is like a dream in that it is a symbolic event which contains sensations, images, and thoughts. It too represents a wish fulfillment. Reveries take place while a person is awake, and are a kind of daydream, an abstract, fanciful musing. Creative thinking, like the other forms of nonlogical thinking, is often fanciful, inventive, and novel. But it is usually closer than reveries to conscious thought because it is more directly concerned with problem solving.

Many people in our society have experienced altered states of consciousness through drugs, transcendental meditation, hypnosis, dreaming, fantasizing, and the like. Much has been written on these altered states of consciousness but it needs to be collected and arranged to show its possible relevance to the study of rhetoric.

It was stated earlier that the Greeks and Romans had two conceptions of the commonplaces and of the memory places. The nonlogical topics seem to be related to Aristotle's notion that the mind thinks in images. Thus the spatial metaphors used by Cicero and Quintilian are not merely fanciful mnemonic devices, but seem to be directly related to one important mode of thinking.

All of the processes of invention articulated in this chapter reveal either explicitly or implicitly some kind of relationship between thinking and writing. The system of topics presented here is obviously tentative and partial. Subsequent research should provide new additions, deletions, rearrangements, and further refinements and delineations of the basic categories. But the main outlines are clear. Much work, however, still remains to be done.

The Composing Process

The process of composing is often thought to be so intuitive and mysterious that any attempt to plumb its mysteries is looked on with disfavor. According to some critics, the process of composition originates in the imagination, and the imagination is not accessible to observation. Other critics believe that the process of composition originates in the rational processes of the mind. As we have seen, however, studies in psychoneurology have shown that both of these views are partial, that the mind has two major modes of consciousness, the rational and the intuitive, and that these modes may operate simultaneously in the normal individual.

Composition is an organic development that begins with a kind of intuitive grasp of the end to be achieved and that concludes when that end is brought to completion. The problem of composing is the problem of how an intention or purpose that is already partially realized in the mind gets what it needs to complete itself. The metaphor which perhaps best describes this process is that of a tree whose potential is already partially realized in the seed. The seed is like the gestalt in the process of invention. It contains within itself everything necessary for a mature development, but unless it is given careful attention and nourishment, it may never reach fruition.

It is not enough that in the process of composing the writer see his subject whole. The writer may know in general the end he wants to achieve without knowing all the details. The gestalt has to be brought to fulfillment, slowly, bit by bit, by linear methods. Thus the process of composing begins with a general idea, but the main process is one of filling in the details. Once the mind intuitively grasps the initial gestalt, then the rational mental processes can take over and the process of composition can proceed in a logical, analytical manner.

Invention always seems to take place within a system. There is always some kind of structure underlying the process. To invent is to extend a system which is already present in the mind. It is possible, of course, that even when operating within a system the mind may fail to express the original conception successfully. If the problem is insufficient information, further research or observation or experiment is needed. Other problems might be caused by attention to the wrong details, or failure to relate the constructs of the system to anything outside the system.

The subconscious mind usually provides the design for the composing process, and the conscious mind provides its development, although the reverse is also possible. Actually, this is an oversimplification since there is a constant interplay between these two modes of consciousness. Since the subconscious part of the mind is not always accessible, the writer must aid the subconscious as much as possible by a deliberate and conscious effort, by defining the problem, by filling in the details, by carefully working out the design, in brief, by preparing the mind so that the subconscious can take over. The old truism that invention favors the well prepared mind seems to be an accurate one.

I have said that invention always takes place within a system or systems. What is this system like? Paradoxically, the topics of invention are both the parts and the whole of this system. At no stage in the composing process can division into parts be separated from classification or classification from comparison. Probably all of the topics operate together as a single entity in the process of composing although for theoretical purposes we can distinguish them. All are manifestations of the same underlying thought processes. Although we categorize them and label them with terms such as "division into parts" or "classification" or "comparison," we are really looking at a single process from different points of view. To divide into parts is to classify, to classify is to compare, and so on *ad infinitum.*

In a rhetorical theory which depends on both competence and performance, it makes sense to isolate each category and to see it as being sufficient in itself to generate discourse, even though in the composing process all of these processes probably operate simultaneously. Thus metaphor alone can be used to generate a discourse. So also can classification or cause and effect.

Notes

1. The following discussion is based in part on these sources: Aristotle, *Rhetorica*, trans. W. Rhys Roberts in *The Works of Aristotle*, vol. 9, ed. W. D. Ross (Oxford: Clarendon Press, 1924); Cicero, *De Inventione* and *Topica*, trans. H. M. Hubbell (Cambridge, Mass. and London: The Loeb Classical Library, 1959); Cicero, *Rhetorica Ad Herennium*, trans. Harry Caplan (London: William Heinemann, Ltd., 1954); Sister Joan Marie Lechner, O. S. U., *Renaissance Concepts of the Commonplaces* (New York: Pageant Press, 1962); Walter J. Ong, S. J., *The Presence of the Word* (New Haven and London: Yale University Press, 1967); Frances A. Yates, *The Art of Memory* (London: Routledge and Kegan Paul, 1966).

2. Michael S. Gazzaniga, *The Bisected Brain* (New York: Appleton-Century-Crofts, 1970), pp. 1–2.

3. Robert E. Ornstein, "Right and Left Thinking," *Psychology Today* (May 1973), pp. 87, 90.

4. Ornstein, pp. 87, 92.

5. Charles W. Telford and James M. Sawrey, *Psychology* (Belmont, Calif.: Brooks/Cole Publishing Co., 1968), p. 250.

6. Emil A. Gutheil, *The Handbook of Dream Analysis* (New York: Liveright Publishing Corp., 1951), pp. 229–231.

V

ARRANGEMENT: SYNTAGMATIC STRUCTURE

Order in composition presents a set of necessary relations that can be precisely described, and this description is the task of the rhetorician. Yet despite the countless number of composition and rhetoric texts dealing with arrangement, we know very little about order in composition. In many texts, arrangement is either neglected, or its treatment is woefully inadequate.

Traditional Approaches

For many writers of traditional classroom texts, a discourse has roughly a beginning, a middle, and an end. However, this kind of organizational advice is so general as to be almost worthless to the beginning writer. Some writers do make a more formal distinction among spatial patterns, temporal patterns, and logical patterns. Quite often these patterns are aligned with the traditional modes of discourse. In this approach, descriptive writing uses spatial patterns; narrative writing uses temporal patterns; and expository writing and argumentation use logical patterns. In some textbooks, there is a further subdivision of the logical patterns into four main types: process, thesis and support, classification, and comparison and contrast. Even when the classification of these patterns is more extensive, as in the so-called "patterns of development" approach, the analysis of the form and structure of these patterns is usually superficial.

In classical rhetoric, rhetoricians dealt with the structure of discourse under the concept of *dispositio* (arrangement). The procedure seems to have been that once students had gathered the ideas obtained through the process of invention, they then had to arrange these ideas in the best possible order. This order sometimes took the following form: the introduction (*exordium*), the statement of fact (*narratio*), the central part of the discourse (*confirmatio*), the refutation of opposing views (*refutatio*), and the conclusion (*peroratio*). In theory, there was a close connection between invention and arrangement, but in practice each was handled as a separate stage in the composing process. Despite its usefulness, the classical pattern of arrangement is considered by many critics to be too mechanical, static, and arbitrary to be of much value today. A more serious charge is that the classical pattern of arrangement is severely limited because it applies primarily to the organization of argumentative discourse; consequently, it is of dubious value when applied to other modes. Although there is much truth in these charges, classical arrangement did at least present a clear pattern of organization for speakers and writers to follow.

Invention and Arrangement

In the conceptual theory of rhetoric, the concept of arrangement is closely connected to that of invention. Following Aristotle's system, I take form to be closely related to the formal principle (i.e., one of the causes of a mode of being) which produces discourse. In other words, in the inventive process, the writer begins with a mental image or plan of the discourse which is to be produced. This image (which is extrinsic to the discourse and represents the efficient cause) corresponds roughly to the order of the discourse itself (which is intrinsic and represents the formal or material cause). The formal principle or process of invention is therefore implicit in any discourse. If, for example, the predominant organizational pattern of a mode of discourse takes the form of a comparison, then the writer must have gone through the inventive process of comparing in order to produce that pattern.

The point of view taken in this study is that the topical categories of definition, partition, classification, enumeration, exemplification, cause and effect, comparison, contrast, and the like, may be considered as formal patterns of arrangement for organizing discourse on almost any level of structure. In this respect, they are similar to the so-called patterns of development found in traditional composition texts, but they differ from them in many important respects. First, as has already been noted, these patterns of development are not only organizational, they are also topical as well; that is, they can be used to serve a heuristic function. Second, they are to be considered dynamic organizational processes, symbolic manifestations of underlying mental processes, and not merely conventional, static patterns. Third, these conceptual patterns are idealizations which the rhetorician is free to abstract from actual discourse. Fourth, they are also to be considered universal patterns of discourse containing structural features which underlie all languages.

Logical Patterns

Since these patterns of discourse are also topical, we would not expect them to differ in kind from the topical categories. Rather than putting these patterns in the same diagrammatic form as the topics, we can emphasize their use as patterns of arrangement by illustrating them graphically as follows:

LOGICAL PATTERNS OF ARRANGEMENT

I. Static Logical Patterns
   A. Description
   B. Definition
   C. Division into Parts
      1. Partition
      2. Enumeration
   D. Classification
   E. Exemplification
   F. Comparison
      1. Similarity
         a. Literal

b. Figurative
2. Difference
   a. Kind
   b. Degree
     1) Greater
     2) Lesser
II. Progressive Logical Patterns
   A. Narration
   B. Process
   C. Cause and Effect
   D. Syllogistic Progression
III. Repetitive Logical Patterns
   A. Iteration
   B. Negation
   C. Alternation

NONLOGICAL PATTERNS OF ARRANGEMENT

   I. Fantasy
   II. Hallucination
   III. Dream
   IV. Reverie
   V. Vision
   VI. Trance
   VII. Meditation

We already know something about the logical patterns of arrangement. Descriptions of many of these patterns, such as partition, classification, exemplification, process, cause and effect, and comparison and contrast, can be found in standard composition texts. But the examples are usually limited, and they contain vague references concerning conceptual processes with few generalizations to explain the types. We need to know much more. We need to know, for example, how these structures manifest themselves as organizational patterns in complete essays as well as in paragraphs. We need more accurate and exhaustive linguistic analyses of these patterns. We need to know more about their rhetorical effects. Finally, we need to know how to make these patterns generative. How can we give our students an understanding of the general principles which underlie discourse while at the same time using particular instances of discourse as examples? And how can we get them to illustrate these principles in their own writing?

Nonlogical Patterns

The nonlogical patterns of arrangement are the most difficult to deal with in our present state of knowledge. Therefore, most of the examples that follow come from literary discourse. Some works that immediately come to mind are: James Joyce's *Ulysses* (stream of consciousness, fantasy), James Thurber's "The Secret Life of Walter Mitty" (daydream, fantasy), Katherine Anne Porter's "Flowering Judas" (dreams), T. S. Eliot's "The Love Song of J. Alfred Prufrock" (stream of consciousness, fantasy), the symbolist poems of Stéphane Mallarmé and Arthur Rimbaud (free association, fantasy, hallucination), Lewis Carroll's *Alice's Adventures in Wonderland* (dreams, free association, punning, transformations), and the poetry of dada and surrealism (free association, transformation, and so on).

Reindividuation

A common criticism that arises when dealing with formal principles in rhetoric is that discourse manifests itself as concrete, particular, and individual, while these formal principles and patterns of arrangement are abstract, general, and universal. How then can they be useful for the study of rhetoric? Their usefulness, according to Kenneth Burke, resides in the fact that these formal patterns can be reindividuated into different subject matter; that is, a particular form can be filled out with a completely different subject matter. As Burke explains it:

> Each word re-embodies the formal principles in different subject matter. A "metaphor" is a concept, an abstraction, but a specific metaphor, exemplified by specific images, is an "individuation." Its appeal as form resides in the fact that its particular subject matter enables the mind to follow a metaphor-process. In this sense we would restore the Platonic relationship between form and matter. A form is a way of experiencing; and such a form is made

available in art when, by the use of specific subject matter, it enables us to experience in this way.[1]

These formal principles recur in all discourse, but they are embodied or individuated in particular subject matter. Burke calls them "innate forms of the mind," a view which coincides with our own theory, which views conceptual patterns of arrangement as symbolizing thought processes. Thus, if we think metaphorically it is because such thinking parallels certain mental processes which are basic to our experience. Therefore, these formal patterns of arrangement are just as surely psychological universals as are the topical categories that they so faithfully reflect. Their external features may change from discourse to discourse, but their essence does not.

I have said that the treatment of arrangement in patterns of discourse beyond the paragraph has been either neglected or woefully inadequate, and that the descriptions purporting to explain these patterns have usually been limited. How best can we approach these formal patterns for purposes of analysis and for subsequent composition? There are two kinds of structural analyses I believe may be useful in describing extended units of discourse beyond the sentence and, more importantly, beyond the paragraph: syntagmatic analysis and paradigmatic analysis.

Syntagmatic analysis is the linguistic analysis of a text which follows the linear order of elements from one sentence to another and from one paragraph to another. Thus, if a discourse consists of five paragraphs, containing a total of 250 sentences, then the structure of the discourse is described in terms of this order. Paradigmatic analysis is the structural analysis of a text in which certain sentences or other linguistic elements are extracted from the sequential order and placed in a schematic pattern or paradigm.

Syntagmatic Analysis

Syntagmatic analysis, though not always referred to by that label, has been used with moderate success by linguists and rhetoricians to describe units of structure beyond the sentence, but so far as I know, very little has been done in describing units of discourse beyond the paragraph. Most notable of these approaches are the following: Zellig

Harris's discourse analysis, Samuel Levin's analysis of linguistic structures in poetry, Francis Christensen's generative rhetoric of the paragraph, Alton Becker's tagmemic approach to paragraph analysis, and Paul Rodger's discourse-centered rhetoric of the paragraph.[2] All of these approaches have their merits, but the kind of syntagmatic analysis I feel will be most beneficial to both teachers and students (because it appears to be the simplest and the one which is relatively free of jargon) is an extension of the methods proposed by Christensen for the analysis of the paragraph.

Michael Grady, a former colleague of Christensen's at Northern Illinois University, has attempted to apply the principles set forth by Christensen to the analysis of the whole composition.[3] According to Grady, every expository essay has an introductory sequence which is roughly comparable to the topic sentence of a paragraph. This introductory sequence is often included in the introductory paragraph (the topic paragraph), but if the essay is long, then the introductory sequence may be expressed in rather general terms. The supporting paragraphs narrow down and add specific details and examples to the basic sequence. "Thus the relation between sections of the body of the paper, and the Introductory Sequence is conceptually the same relationship that holds between the subsequent sentences in a paragraph, and the topic sentence of that paragraph."[4]

Grady's position has some merit. My own approach to discourse analysis, however, is one that conceives of units larger than the paragraph as primarily sequences of structurally related sentences (i.e., a group of sentences which are related to each other by coordination and subordination), and secondarily as a sequence of structurally related paragraphs.

In this view, the essay is a kind of macroparagraph. The first sentence of the essay (or extended discourse) is the organizing sentence. (I shall call it the *lead sentence* to distinguish it from the traditional concept of the thesis sentence.) The lead sentence is the top sentence of the sequence; it is the sentence that gets the discourse going. Subsequent sentences in the discourse are related to it by coordination or subordination.

The method for analyzing the structure of an extended discourse is very similar to that proposed by Francis Christensen for analyzing the structure of a paragraph. But it also is related to the kind of paragraph analysis proposed by Paul Rodgers. According to Rodgers:

Paragraph structure is part and parcel of the structure of the discourse as a whole; a given stadium becomes a paragraph not by virtue of its structure but because the writer elects to indent, his indentation functioning, as does all punctuation, as a gloss upon the overall literary process under way at that point. Paragraphs are not composed; they are discovered. To compose is to create; to indent is to interpret.[5]

Rodgers contends that there are many reasons for indenting a new paragraph. The paragraph may in fact shift to a new idea. But oftentimes the writer decides to indent because of a change in tone, because of a shift in the rhythm, because of emphasis, or because of purely formal considerations. Christensen claims that he is always conscious of paragraphing when he writes. Rodgers asserts that he usually goes back after he has completed his writing to make his paragraph indentations. Surely the truth lies somewhere between. We invent paragraphs, and we discover paragraphs. At times we are highly conscious of the reasons for indenting a particular group of words as a paragraph; at times we are not.

The procedure for analyzing the structure of an extended discourse along the lines indicated above is relatively simple. The reader assumes provisionally that the opening sentence of the essay is the lead sentence. Then he proceeds, sentence by sentence, through the whole discourse, searching for similarities and differences. If the second sentence is like the first, then it is set down as coordinate and given the same number as the first sentence. If the second sentence differs from the first, then it is indented as being subordinate to the first, and it is given the number 2. If the third sentence differs from the second, it too is indented and given the next number, but if it is coordinate to the previous sentence, then it is given the same number. A sentence may be either subordinate or coordinate to the sentence immediately above it.

The method of determining coordination and subordination between sentences is not always clear in Christensen's analyses of paragraph structure, which often seem to be based on an intuitive sense of semantic relationships between sentences. However, there are a number of ways of determining these relationships, many of which are well known to teachers and scholars. There are two main kinds of subordination between sentences: grammatical subordination and semantic subordination. Some typical examples of grammatical subordination include: the use of a pronoun in one sentence to refer to a noun in the previous sentence; the use of transitional markers such as *therefore, nevertheless, thus,* and the like, to tie sentences together; the repetition of a word or a part of a word (based on the same root) in a subsequent sentence to link it to a similar word in the previous sentence; and the use of a synonym to refer to an equivalent word in a previous sentence. Semantic relationships are much more difficult to discern, but in general these relationships are determined by noting the deductive or inductive movement of the meaning relationships in a discourse. Thus a sentence which gives an example, a reason, a statistic, a fact, or a detail is considered to be subordinate to a more general statement which preceded it.

Like subordination, coordination between sentences may be grammatical or semantic. One of the clearest signs of grammatical coordination is parallel structure as, for example, in anaphoric repetition. More often than not, grammatical coordination will contain semantic coordination, as in antithetical sentences, but if grammatical clues (for example, the repetition of similar syntactic structures such as nominals, prepositional phrases, or various kinds of clauses) are not present, then another way of determining semantic coordination is by looking for semantic groupings of examples, reasons, details, and considering sentences which contain these groupings as coordinate. Clearly, much more work has to be done in delineating ways of determining relationships between sentences, but these examples do illustrate some of the more important methods.

Each sentence is considered in turn, indented as subordinate or set down as coordinate. Enough space is left between the last sentence of this paragraph and the first sentence of the following paragraph so that the paragraph division becomes apparent. This procedure is followed for each succeeding paragraph.

Discourse Analysis

The following analysis of a news article by Carl P. Leubsdorf, entitled "Contrasts Divide Goldwater Race and McGovern's," which appeared in *The Arizona Republic* on Friday, July 14, 1972, is an example of this kind of descriptive approach:

CONTRASTS DIVIDE GOLDWATER RACE
AND MCGOVERN'S
By Carl P. Leubsdorf
Associated Press

I

1 Republicans hope, and many Democrats fear, that Democratic presidential nominee George McGovern is a Barry Goldwater of the left, an extremist doomed to defeat so overwhelming he will carry much of his party down with him.

2

2 Parallels do exist with Goldwater, the conservative GOP nominee routed in 1964 by Lyndon B. Johnson, but the contrasts appear to be far more striking as McGovern sets out to unify the Democrats to challenge President Nixon in November.

3

3 Like Goldwater, the liberal McGovern started with the narrow support of what was considered an extreme fringe of his party.

3 Like Goldwater, he is a pleasant man, with support from devoted followers.

4

3 As they did for Goldwater, supporters of McGovern packed the caucuses and state conventions to squeeze delegate representation often far beyond their real support among voters.

5

3 And like Goldwater, McGovern became leader of a deeply divided party with many key figures saying he not only couldn't win but meant party disaster.

6

2 Beyond the superficial, however, the differences between Goldwater and McGovern are broad and basic.

7
3 Goldwater was carried by his followers to a presidential nomination he never really wanted.
    4 He regarded politics as an unpleasant chore.

8
3 McGovern, behind that blend of professor and preacher, is a politician who got his start by building a South Dakota Democratic Party that was basically a vehicle for electing George McGovern to Congress.

9
3 McGovern wants to be president, is determined to achieve his goal and confident he can.

10
    4 He represents the nation's majority party that, even while divided, gives him a far stronger starting point than the divided and minority GOP gave Goldwater eight years ago.

11
3 Goldwater's nomination was fashioned in the confines of caucuses and conventions.
    4 His primary record was weak until he squeaked through against Nelson A. Rockefeller in California.

12
3 McGovern's nomination is the product of political reforms that have made primary elections the dominant feature of the process.
    4 Starting with a close run against Edmund S. Muskie in New Hampshire and a break-through in Wisconsin, McGovern swept victoriously through the last seven Democratic primaries and amassed two-thirds of his delegates at the polls.

13

3 Goldwater was an idealogue, a man willing, even eager, to articulate and emphasize controversial positions even if it meant antagonizing large segments of his party.

14

3 McGovern envisions himself as a unifier.

    4 Over the past month, he has sought to tone down his more controversial positions to increase their acceptability to potential rivals.

15

3 Goldwater sought the presidency when one president, John F. Kennedy, had just been assassinated, and his successor, Lyndon B. Johnson, was riding a wave of sympathy and support as he achieved success with a friendly Congress.

16

3 McGovern runs when the president is Richard M. Nixon.

    4 While riding high after highly publicized trips to Peking and Moscow, he is still a disliked figure to a generation of Democrats who have fought him in five of the past six national campaigns.

17

2 Then, there are the issues.

18

3 Goldwater was cast, partly through his own statements, as the hawk in a nation of doves, the man who would escalate U.S. involvement in Vietnam, against whom Johnson could campaign as the candidate of peace.

19

3 McGovern claims to have been "right from the start" on the central national political issue of the decade, the Vietnam War.

    4 His opposition to the war has been at the heart of his public positions.

20
2 Is McGovern a Goldwater?

21
3 When the Arizona senator ran, he became the major issue of that campaign.
  4 Political oratory revolved around his views, whether they were dangerous for the country.

22
3 In the last six weeks, political oratory has increasingly revolved around McGovern's proposals.
  4 In California, this played a crucial part as Hubert H. Humphrey closed with a rush after polls had showed him a sure loser.

23
3 Similarly, in the fall campaign, President Nixon and his campaigners will seek to make McGovern the issue.

24
3 The South Dakota senator, in turn, will seek to make Nixon's credibility the issue.

25
  4 Whether he succeeds or is forced to spend the next four months defending his record may determine whether McGovern meets Goldwater's fate.

This kind of analysis reveals a number of interesting things: the overall structure of the discourse, the organization of the paragraphs in relation to the larger structure of the discourse, the structural relationship of the sentences, and the logical presentation of the comparison.

As a macroparagraph, this essay is organized in much the same way as the "cumulative" paragraph, and it exemplifies the same structural principles. It is a sequence of sentences related to one another by coordination and subordination. The first sentence is the *lead sentence;* it acts as the organizing sentence of the entire discourse. The second sentence, which constitutes a new paragraph, is subordinate to the first. Sentences 3 and 4, which together comprise the third paragraph, are parallel structures which are coordinate to each other, but subordinate to the previous sentence. Sentences 5 and 6, each of which is a separate paragraph (paragraphs 4 and 5) are coordinate to each other and to the previous two sentences, but they are subordinate to sentence 2. Sentence 7 (paragraph 6), since it repeats a parallel idea, is coordinate to sentence 2. The remaining sentences are organized in much the same way as the previous sentences, that is, they are related to each other by subordination or coordination.

If we next consider the discourse not merely as a group of structurally related sentences, but also as a sequence of structurally related paragraphs, we discover that the essay consists of twenty-five paragraphs, varying in length from one to two sentences (no paragraph is longer than two sentences) and from four words to fifty-four words. As a way of illustrating paragraph length, I have numbered the paragraphs consecutively from one to twenty-five, and I have included the total number of words contained in each paragraph in parentheses: 1 (36); 2 (39); 3 (32); 4 (26); 5 (25); 6 (14); 7 (21); 8 (33); 9 (15); 10 (28); 11 (26); 12 (54); 13 (25); 14 (28); 15 (38); 16 (43); 17 (5); 18 (35); 19 (35); 20 (4); 21 (26); 22 (36); 23 (17); 24 (14); 25 (22). The average number of words in each paragraph is 26.9. The average number of words in each sentence is 19.9. There is a total of 34 sentences in the discourse.

When we consider the relative length of the sentences and of the paragraphs in relationship to the length of the sentences and paragraphs in other discourses, we cannot help but notice the paragraph divisions and wonder what basis has been used for making them. Is it logical, psychological, formal, or merely arbitrary? The logical basis seems to be the weakest, in my opinion. In terms of the conceptual structure of the comparison, I would consider paragraph 1 as a single unit, but I would group paragraphs 2, 3, 4, and 5 as a single paragraph; paragraphs 6, 7, 8, 9, 10, 11, 12, 13, 14, 15, and 16 as a unit; 17, 18, and 19 as another unit; and 20, 21, 22, 23, 24, and 25 as a final unit.

The opening paragraph sets up the basic antithesis ("Republicans hope/many Democrats fear") and thus logically could stand alone as a complete unit. Paragraphs 2, 3, 4, and 5 constitute another logical unit, dealing with the similarities that exist between Goldwater and McGovern, and these paragraphs could be structured as a single paragraph. In addition to the controlling idea, unity and coherence is further achieved by the repetition of parallel structures ("like Goldwater," "like Goldwater," "as they did for Goldwater," "and like Goldwater") at the beginning of the successive sentences, all referring back to the base clause, "parallels do exist with Goldwater." In fact it appears that all of the sentences marked level 2 could begin new paragraphs. The logical basis of the subsequent units would be the differences that exist between Goldwater and McGovern. In turn, each paragraph dealing with differences has a separate semantic basis. Paragraphs 6 through 16 (now considered as one unit) are based on "broad and basic" differences. Paragraphs 17, 18, and 19 revolve around "the issues." And paragraphs 20 through 25 deal with the personalities of the two candidates.

So there could be a logical regrouping of the existing paragraphs into larger paragraph units, but the writer has decided, ostensibly for other reasons, to group his sentences into different units. This suggests that, at least in this discourse, Rodgers' view is valid, that is, that the paragraphs may have been discovered rather than invented.

The fact that this article appeared in a newspaper suggests some reasons for the paragraph divisions. In many newspaper articles, the sentences and the paragraphs tend to be short. There are both psychological and formal reasons for this kind of structuring, among them the educational level of the mass audience, the neat, orderly appearance that such a format presents, the readability of the paragraphs, and the balance achieved by making the paragraphs the same average length.

If we regroup the sentences into new paragraph units as suggested above, the resultant structure would appear as follows:

1

1 Republicans hope, and many Democrats fear, that Democratic presidential nominee George McGovern is a Barry Goldwater of the left, an extremist doomed to defeat so overwhelming he will carry much of his party down with him.

2

2 Parallels do exist with Goldwater, the conservative GOP nominee routed in 1964 by Lyndon B. Johnson, but the contrasts appear to be far more striking as McGovern sets out to unify the Democrats to challenge President Nixon in November.

3 Like Goldwater, the liberal McGovern started with the narrow support of what was considered an extreme fringe of his party.

3 Like Goldwater, he is a pleasant man, with support from devoted followers.

3 As they did for Goldwater, supporters of McGovern packed the caucuses and state conventions to squeeze delegate representation often far beyond their real support among voters.

3 And like Goldwater, McGovern became leader of a deeply divided party with many key figures saying he not only couldn't win but meant party disaster.

3

2 Beyond the superficial, however, the differences between Goldwater and McGovern are broad and basic.

3 Goldwater was carried by his followers to a presidential nomination he never really wanted.

4 He regarded politics as an unpleasant chore.

3 McGovern, behind that blend of professor and preacher, is a politician who got his start by building a South Dakota Democratic Party that was basically a vehicle for electing George McGovern to Congress.

3 McGovern wants to be president, is determined to achieve his goal, and confident he can win.

4 He represents the nation's majority party that, even while divided, gives him a far stronger starting point than the divided and minority GOP gave Goldwater eight years ago.

3 Goldwater's nomination was fashioned in the confines of caucuses and conventions.

4 His primary record was weak until he squeaked through against Nelson A. Rockefeller in California.

3 McGovern's nomination is the product of political reforms that have made primary elections the dominant feature of the process.

4 Starting with a close run against Edmund S. Muskie in New Hampshire and a break-through in Wisconsin, McGovern swept victoriously through the last

seven Democratic primaries and amassed two-thirds of his delegates at the polls.

3 Goldwater was an idealogue, a man willing, even eager, to articulate and emphasize controversial positions even if it meant antagonizing large segments of his party.

3 McGovern envisions himself as a unifier.

    4 Over the past month, he has sought to tone down his more controversial positions to increase their acceptability to potential rivals.

3 Goldwater sought the presidency when one president, John F. Kennedy, had just been assassinated, and his successor, Lyndon B. Johnson, was riding a wave of sympathy and support as he achieved success after success with a friendly Congress.

3 McGovern runs when the president is Richard M. Nixon.

    4 While riding high after highly publicized trips to Peking and Moscow, he is still a disliked figure to a generation of Democrats who have fought him in five of the past six national campaigns.

4

2 Then, there are the issues.

3 Goldwater was cast, partly through his own statements, as the hawk in a nation of doves, the man who would escalate U.S. involvement in Vietnam, against whom Johnson could campaign as the candidate of peace.

3 McGovern claims to have been "right from the start" on the central national political issue of the decade, the Vietnam War.

    4 His opposition to the war has been at the heart of his public positions.

5

2 Is McGovern a Goldwater?

3 When the Arizona senator ran, he became the major issue of that campaign.

    4 Political oratory revolved around his views, whether they were dangerous for the country.

3 In the last six weeks, political oratory has increasingly revolved around McGovern's proposals.
   4 In California, this played a crucial part as Hubert
   H. Humphrey closed with a rush after polls had
   showed him a sure loser.
3 Similarly, in the fall campaign, President Nixon and his
campaigners will seek to make McGovern the issue.
3 The South Dakota senator, in turn, will seek to make
Nixon's credibility the issue.
   4 Whether he succeeds or is forced to spend the next
   four months defending his record may determine
   whether McGovern meets Goldwater's fate.

Arrangement and Delivery

This new alignment of the sentences and paragraphs clearly indicates that there is more to paragraphing than many conventional texts
would have us believe. Surely the rhetorical effect of this new structure
differs from that of the old. More importantly, this kind of analysis
suggests that there may be a closer relationship between arrangement
and delivery than previously supposed. Arrangement (*dispositio*) is that
part of rhetoric concerned with the organization of a discourse. Delivery
(*pronuntiatio*) is the division of rhetoric concerned with the manner
in which a discourse is presented. Naturally, with the invention of
printing and with the appearance of written discourse, delivery was
neglected. But if we conceive of delivery in written discourse as the way
in which a writer attempts to present the text in the most effective
manner, clearly the relationship between delivery and arrangement takes
on a new meaning. An orator can use modulations and inflections of
the voice, gestures, and other mannerisms, while a writer must use
spelling, punctuation, indentations, and all of those devices that we
usually associate with format. If this approach to delivery in writing
seems too artificial, we should recall how effectively poets such as e.e.
cummings have used these techniques in their own writing to please,
to instruct, to move, or to persuade their readers.

Notes

1. Kenneth Burke, *Counter-Statement,* 2nd ed. (Los Altos, California: Hermes Publications, 1953), p. 143.

2. A. L. Becker, "A Tagmemic Approach to Paragraph Analysis," *College Composition and Communication,* XVI (December 1965), 237–242; Francis Christensen, "A Generative Rhetoric of the Paragraph," *College Composition and Communication,* XIV (October 1965), 144–156; Zellig S. Harris, "Discourse Analysis" in *The Structure of Language,* eds. Jerry A. Fodor and Jerrold J. Katz (Englewood Cliffs, N.J.: Prentice-Hall, Inc., 1964), pp. 355–383; Samuel R. Levin, *Linguistic Structures in Poetry* (The Hague: Mouton and Co., 1962); Paul C. Rodgers, Jr., "A Discourse-Centered Rhetoric of the Paragraph," *College Composition and Communication,* XVII (February 1966), 2–11.

3. Michael Grady, "A Conceptual Rhetoric of the Composition," *College Composition and Communication,* XXII (December 1971), 348–354; "On Teaching Christensen Rhetoric," *English Journal,* 61 (September 1972), 859–873, 877.

4. "On Teaching Christensen Rhetoric," p. 864.

5. Rodgers, p. 43.

VI

ARRANGEMENT: PARADIGMATIC STRUCTURE

Syntagmatic analysis is based on text progression; paradigmatic analysis is based on repetition within a text. The first may be considered temporal, the second, spatial. Both kinds of analyses are important for the study of rhetoric, for as has often been pointed out, the two planes of language are interdependent. Syntagms contain elements of paradigms, and paradigms consist of elements of syntagms. Each kind of analysis constitutes a different point of view.

Antecedents

Paradigmatic linguistic analysis has been used by traditional grammarians to study the declensions of nouns and the conjugations of verbs and by the structuralists to compare the inflected and derivational forms of affixes and bases and to classify the form class words. But the application of paradigmatic linguistic analysis to the study of discourse seems to have evolved from the techniques used by linguists, anthropologists, and literary critics to study recurring patterns in myth, folklore, poetry, and prose fiction.[1] No one, to my knowledge, has used this kind

74

of analysis to study the patterns of expository or persuasive discourse. One of the earliest proponents of paradigmatic analysis was Claude Lévi-Strauss who has applied the insights of structural linguistics to the study of myth. Lévi-Strauss's technique consists essentially of taking a myth and breaking it down into "the shortest possible sentences." This technique has the effect of "normalizing" the text since there is no attempt to use the original sentences of the text. The sentences thus consist of a kind of text paraphrase, although the derived sentences seem to correspond very closely to the kernel sentences of transformational grammar. Each sentence isolated by Lévi-Strauss contains a particular action (or function) which is linked to a particular subject. Lévi-Strauss calls these sentences "gross constituent units." Once the sentences have been isolated, they are placed on an index card so that the structure of the myth becomes apparent. Thus a partial structure of a particular version of the Oedipus myth might look like this:

1 Kadmos seeks
   his sister Europa,
   ravished by Zeus

                                2 Kadmos kills
                                    the dragon

               3 The Spartoi kill
                 each other
               4 Oedipus kills
                 his father, Laios

                                5 Oedipus kills
                                  the Sphinx.

6 Oedipus marries
   his mother, Jocasta
               7 Eteocles kills
                 his brother, Polynices

The resultant scheme presents the basic units of the myth on two different planes: the diachronic or temporal which illustrates text progression (as represented by the numbered sequence) and the synchronic or spatial which constitutes the underlying paradigm (the vertical plane). Since a myth is made up of all of its variants, the next step is to consider each variant in turn, using the same kind of analysis and placing the gross constituent units of each variant on a separate card. When a sufficient number of different versions of the same myth have been analyzed and compared, the assertions common to all of these versions will constitute a kind of prototype or archetype of a particular myth.

An important assumption of Lévi-Strauss's position is that a linear analysis of a text is not sufficient to reveal the essential characteristics of a myth. The linear, sequential structure of a text reveals only the surface or manifest content, whereas the spatial, paradigmatic structure reveals the underlying or latent content. The underlying structure, according to Lévi-Strauss, is the more important of the two levels.

The techniques used by Propp in the analysis of fairy tales and those used by the Russian formalist critics to analyze prose fiction might more properly be considered syntagmatic structural analysis, since the structure of a particular text is described in terms of the chronological order of sentence progression. But the results of these analyses correspond in many ways to the results of a paradigmatic analysis.

For example, Propp breaks down a particular text into what he calls "functions" or assertions. These functions are then arrayed in chronological order so that the structure of a particular tale stands out. Although the structure is represented in terms of the linear sequence, it is still possible to abstract the underlying paradigm by comparing various tales, for Propp maintains that the structure of all fairy tales is essentially the same. A look at the following example submitted by Propp should make this point a bit clearer (I have rearranged the assertions slightly to make them coincide with the schema presented by Lévi-Strauss):

1	A tsar gives an eagle to a hero	1	The eagle carries the hero away to another kingdom
2	An old man gives Sučenko a horse	2	The horse carries Sučenko away to another kingdom
3	A sorcerer gives Iván a little boat	3	The boat takes Iván to another kingdom
4	A princess gives Iván a ring	4	Young men . . . carry Iván away into another kingdom

Although the names and the attributes of the various characters change from tale to tale, their actions (giving, carrying away to another kingdom) remain constant. It is these actions that constitute the basic elements of the tale and that can be abstracted to reveal the underlying structure.

Tomashevsky, in his study of prose fiction, divides his text into what he calls *motifs*. A motif is a segment of a text which has a basic subject–verb or subject–verb–object pattern. In this respect a motif is very much like the kernel sentence of transformational grammar or the gross constituent unit of Claude Lévi-Strauss. A motif may be an actual sentence of the text, or it may be a sentence which summarizes some part of the text. Some typical examples of motifs in *Crime and Punishment*, according to Tomashevsky, are "evening came," "Raskolnikov killed the old woman," "the hero died." The actual wording of the motif does not seem to be as important as the text content which the motif summarizes. Tomashevsky's basic structural unit differs from that of Propp in that Propp is more interested in recurring motif functions which are common to all fairy tales, whereas Tomashevsky is more concerned with the motif as a unit in the structure of a particular literary work.

In his article, "Toward a Structural Theory of Content in Prose Fiction," Lubomír Doležel extends the work of the folklorists and the Russian formalist critics in an interesting new direction. In his analyses of prose fiction, he is interested not only in motif configurations and plot constructions, as the following schema of the second scene of Hemingway's "The Killers" indicates,

NICK'S WALK
Nick's meeting with Mrs. Bell
Nick's entry
Nick's meeting with Ole Anderson
Nick's departure
Nick's meeting with Mrs. Bell
NICK'S WALK

but he is also interested in the abstract formulas which underlie action, scene, and character in prose fiction. One way of rendering the underlying structure of the action in a story might be by means of the following formulas:

A performed an action affecting B.
A performed an action.
A was affected by an action.

Another would be to reduce the formula of a specific motif to abstract symbols. Thus the basic formula of the motif "The hero killed the dragon" could be expressed as "Agent–Action–Patient." The motif "The villain was defeated" could be rendered as "Patient–Actor," that of "The older brother went to the south" as "Modifier–Agent–Action–Modifier," and so forth.

Doležel's most important contention is that any text theory must account for the structure of content. To Doležel, content is "an aspect of text structure." To get at the structure of content, Doležel suggests that one follow a sequence of operations which he depicts graphically in the following scheme:

original text:	expression	meaning
semantic paraphrase:	synonymic expression	equivalent meaning
content paraphrase: (a) *uncondensed:*	transformed expression	referentially equivalent meaning content
(b) *condensed:*	condensed expression	condensed content

In deriving a content paraphrase of the original text, one merely rewrites the original text as a sequence of simple sentence structures (similar to the kernel sentences of transformational grammar). In the process of paraphrasing, more abstract class terms can be substituted for the original words. The main point to remember is that the paraphrase need not be exactly equivalent to the original text, but only referentially equivalent; that is, both the original text and the paraphrase must point to the same referent. The final step is to reduce the uncondensed paraphrase (which has been rewritten as a sequence of simple sentences) to a condensed paraphrase. The degree of condensation depends on the nature of the text as well as ones purpose. The condensed paraphrase can be arrived at either by combining several sentences into one condensed sentence or by abstracting key sentences "by using a certain formal or semantic criterion of relevance."

Although most of the studies dealing with paradigmatic analyses have been primarily concerned with imaginative discourse, many of these techniques, it seems to me, could be useful in analyzing nonfiction discourse.

In the conceptual theory of rhetoric, the paradigmatic level of discourse might be equated to what I have been referring to as the conceptual structure of a discourse. It is the underlying organizational pattern found in complete essays as well as in paragraphs. It is roughly the equivalent of the latent content that Lévi-Strauss maintains underlies myth. It is different, however, in that these paradigms bear a very close resemblance to the so-called patterns of development found in traditional composition texts, such as definition, classification, partition, exemplification, enumeration, and the like.

These paradigms, as I have previously pointed out, are heuristic as well as organizational, that is, they are related to the topics of invention. In addition, they are to be considered as dynamic organizational processes, not merely static conventional patterns. Furthermore, as we have noted, these conceptual patterns are idealizations which the rhetorician is free to abstract from actual discourse. He can do this by using the sentences of a text, by "normalizing" the sentences of the text, or by paraphrasing a segment of the text. Finally, these conceptual patterns (or at least their abstract representations) are to be considered universal patterns of discourse containing structural features which underlie all languages.

The syntagmatic level of discourse manifests itself as being concrete, particular, and unique. The paradigmatic level of discourse corresponds to the underlying formal principles which are abstract, general, and universal. These formal principles can be "re-individuated," in Kenneth Burke's term, in different subject matter and can thus be made generative in producing discourse. The mind embodies these formal principles in its organizational patterns. Thus form in discourse is both the informing principle as well as the shape or structure.

The best way to get at these underlying conceptual patterns is to use a combination of syntagmatic and paradigmatic analyses. Since syntagms contain elements of paradigms and since paradigms are embedded in complete discourses, the most logical approach is to begin with a syntagmatic analysis of the discourse, using the methods suggested in the previous chapter. The reader will find that even at this stage of the analysis, paradigms begin to manifest themselves. The next step is to apply a paradigmatic analysis, and again the procedure used is relatively simple. The reader proceeds, sentence by sentence, through the discourse, looking for instances of semantic and/or syntactic repetition. Not just any instances of repetition will do, however; only those which seem to be related to the conceptual pattern under consideration. Thus, in an enumeration theme, sentences which relate to the pattern of enumeration are abstracted. It is not necessary, as in one of the preliminary stages of

Doležel's text paraphrases, to account for every sentence in the text. Only key sentences (those that Doležel maintains can be arrived at "by using a certain formal or semantic criterion of relevance") should be abstracted and put into a paradigm, and these key sentences would represent the underlying conceptual pattern. In the process of analysis, the analyst should try to use the original sentences of the text whenever possible. If it is necessary to regularize the text, however, for the sake of revealing the underlying paradigm more clearly, then the sentence can be recast in a simpler form using transformational analysis (for example, changing a passive sentence to an active one) or by using a sentence paraphrase. It is not absolutely necessary to reduce each sentence to its kernel form, only to put it into a suitable form that will reveal the basic paradigm.

The resultant paradigm will not only reveal the core structure of a particular kind of pattern of development (a classification paradigm or a comparison paradigm); more importantly, it will reveal the *underlying principle of forward motion,* the plan by which the discourse moves from its beginning to its goal. It is in this sense that these paradigms are related to the topics of invention. They are heuristic insofar as they aid in the invention of ideas. It is in this sense that these paradigms are also generative for once the writer grasps the underlying principles, they can be re-embodied in the inventive process and in organizational patterns.

To illustrate this descriptive approach, I would like to analyze the following discourse by C. L. Wrenn, entitled "General Character of English." It appears in the introduction of Wrenn's book, *The English Language,* and constitutes Section 2 of the introduction. Furthermore, it is indented and labeled as a separate section so that we do a minimum of violence to its integrity in considering it as a separate essay.

GENERAL CHARACTER OF ENGLISH

I

1 The English language is spoken or read by the largest number of people in the world, for historical, political and economic reasons; but it may also be true that it owes something of its wide appeal to qualities and characteristics inherent in itself.

    2 What are these characteristic features which outstand in making the English language what it is, which give it its individuality and make it of this worldwide significance?

3 Some of the more obvious of these are the following.

4 First and most important is its extraordinary receptive and adaptable heterogeneousness—the varied ease and readiness with which it has taken to itself material from almost everywhere in the world and has made the new elements of language its own.

5 English, which when the Anglo-Saxons first conquered England in the fifth and sixth centuries was almost a 'pure' or unmixed language—which could make new words for new ideas from its own compounded elements and had hardly any foreign words—has become the most 'mixed' of languages, having received throughout its history all kinds of foreign elements with ease and assimilated them all to its own character.

6 Though its copiousness of vocabulary is outstanding, it is its amazing variety and heterogeneousness which is even more striking: and this general receptiveness of new elements has contributed to making it a suitable and attractive vehicle in so many parts of the world.

2

4 A second outstanding characteristic of English is its simplicity of inflexion—the ease with which it indicates the relationships of words in a sentence with only the minimum of change in their shapes or variation of endings.

5 There are languages such as Chinese that have surpassed English in the reduction of the language in the matter of inflexions to what looks like just a series of fixed monosyllabic roots; but among European languages taken as a whole English has gone as far as any in reducing the inflexions it once had to a minimum.

6 A natural consequence of this simplifying of inflexion by reduction, however, is that since the relationship of words to each other is no longer made clear by their endings, this must be done in other ways.

3
4 A third quality of English, therefore, is its relatively fixed word-order.

    5 An inflected language like Latin or Russian can afford to be fairly free in the arrangement of its words, since the inflexions show clearly the proper relationship in the sentence, and ambiguity is unlikely.

    5 But in a language which does not change the forms of its words according to their relationship in the sentence-significance, the order of the words is likely to be relatively fixed; and a fixed word order in relation to meaning in the sentence takes the place of the freedom made possible by the system of inflexions.

4
4 Another consequence, fourthly, of the loss or reduction to the minimum of the inflexions which English once had, is the growth of the use of periphrases or roundabout ways of saying things, and of the use of prepositions to take the place of the lost inflexions.

    5 The English simplified verb uses periphrases and compound tenses made with auxiliary verbs to replace the more elaborate system of tenses that once existed (though tenses had already become fairly simple before the Anglo-Saxons came to England).

    5 Similarly, English, which once had nearly as many case endings as Latin, has come to use prepositions instead of these, as can easily be seen if one translates any piece of Latin into English.

5
4 A fifth quality of English—though this, like the loss of inflexions and its consequences, is shared with some other languages—is the development of new varieties of intonation to express shades of meaning which were formerly indicated by varying the shapes of words.

    5 This is perhaps somewhat comparable (though

only in a small way) to the vast use of intonation in Chinese as a method of expressing meaning in sentences which would otherwise seem like series of unvarying monosyllabic roots.

    6 Consider, for instance, the wonderful variety of shades of meaning we may put into the use of the word 'do,' merely by varying the intonation—that is the pitch and intensity, the tone of the voice.

6

2 Not all the above qualities are in themselves necessarily good, nor have they all contributed to the general success of English.

2 But it seems probable that of them all it is the adaptable receptiveness and the simplicity of inflexion that have done most in this regard.

    3 On the other hand, the very copiousness of English leads to vagueness or lack of clarity.

       4 Its resources are too vast for all but the well educated to use to full advantage; and such phenomena as 'pidgin English,' 'journalese,' jargon, woolliness of expression, and slatternly speech and writing, are everywhere likely to be met with.

       5 It may fairly be said that English is among the easiest languages to speak badly, but the most difficult to use well.

Syntagmatic Analysis

This discourse consists of six paragraphs. If we consider the discourse as a sequence of structurally related sentences, then we can tentatively accept the first sentence of the discourse as the *lead sentence*. This is the sentence that acts as the organizing sentence of the entire discourse. The second sentence, since it shows no evidence of grammatical parallelism with the first, is subordinate to the first, the subordination being based on lexical repetition ("characteristics," "characteristic"). Sentence 3 narrows down the idea contained in 2 ("the characteristic features which outstand in making the English language what it is") and helps to further organize the discourse. This sentence is subordinate to sentence 2 on the basis of referential subordination (the word "some" referring to the word "features"). Sentence 4 (which enumerates the first characteristic of the English language that makes it outstand) is subordinate to sentence 3. Sentence 5 narrows down and explains more fully the ways in which the English language has assimilated new elements from other languages, thus making it subordinate to sentence 4. Finally, sentence 6 qualifies the idea contained in the previous sentence ("though its copiousness of vocabulary is outstanding"), making it subordinate to sentence 5.

On the basis of similarity of syntactic structure and on the basis of the enumeration sequence, sentence 7, the first sentence of the second paragraph ("A second outstanding characteristic of English is . . .") is coordinate to sentence 4 in the previous paragraph ("First and foremost is . . ."). Sentence 8, which takes up the idea of "simplicity of inflexion" initiated by sentence 7, is subordinate to it. Sentence 9 qualifies the idea of "this simplifying of inflexion by reduction" and is therefore subordinate to sentence 8.

The first sentence of paragraph 3, sentence 10 ("A third quality of English, therefore, is . . ."), on the basis of grammatical parallelism, is coordinate to both sentences 4 and 7. This sentence also continues the enumeration sequence. Sentence 11 (which considers the idea of the free arrangement of words in an inflected language) is subordinate to sentence 10. Sentence 12 is coordinate to sentence 11 because it considers a parallel but contrasting idea of sentence 11 (the idea of a relatively fixed arrangement of words in a noninflected language). Syntactic parallelism between these two sentences is signalled by the sentence connector "but."

In paragraph 4, sentence 13 ("Another consequence, fourthly . . . is . . .") is parallel to sentences 4, 7, and 10 in each of the previous paragraphs, displaying the same grammatical structure (noun phrase–copula–noun phrase) while at the same time advancing the conceptual pattern of enumeration and division into parts. Sentence 14, which is subordinate to sentence 13, is linked to it on the basis of lexical repetition ("periphrases"). Sentence 15 is coordinate to sentence 14, with syntactic parallelism being signalled by the adverbial "similarly."

Sentence 16, the initial sentence of paragraph 5 ("A fifth quality of English . . . is . . .") further advances the enumeration pattern and is coordinate to sentences 4, 7, 10, and 13. Sentence 17 is subordinate to 16 by referential subordination (the pronoun "this" referring to the phrase, "the development of new varieties of intonation"), and sentence 18, which narrows down and gives a particular example of "variety in shades of meaning using intonation," is subordinate to sentence 17 and is tied to this sentence by the transitional expression, "for instance."

The first two sentences of the last paragraph, sentence 19 ("Not all of the above qualities are in themselves necessarily good . . .") and sentence 20 ("But it seems probable that of them all it is . . ."), are semantically parallel to sentence 3 of the first paragraph ("What are these characteristic features which outstand . . ."). These sentences are co-ordinate to each other as well as to sentence 3. Sentence 21, which is linked to sentence 20 by the expression "on the other hand," is subordinate to it. Sentence 22 is tied in to sentence 21 by referential subordination (with the word "its" referring to the word "English"). Finally, sentence 23, the last sentence of the discourse, is subordinate to sentence 22 by referential subordination. (The word "English" refers to the word "its" in the previous sentence.)

The paragraph divisions have, for the most part, a logical basis. Paragraph 1, however, could be divided into two separate paragraphs. The first three sentences are the organizing sentences of the entire discourse and could therefore be grouped as a single paragraph. The next three sentences (4, 5, and 6), because they all refer to the same idea, could logically be placed in a separate paragraph. The sentences in paragraph 2 can be considered as constituting a thought unit. In fact, with the exception of the first paragraph and the last paragraph, all of the paragraphs which constitute the "body" of the discourse can be considered self-contained logical units. Each of these paragraphs enumerates an outstanding characteristic of the English language. The last paragraph qualifies the ideas in the previous paragraphs and repeats the initial idea of the opening paragraph, thus constituting a kind of "return to the beginning."

The rhetorical pattern of the discourse as a whole may be described as question and answer. The conceptual pattern is that of logical analysis (a combination of division into parts and enumeration).

Paradigmatic Analysis

The logical basis of the paragraph divisions together with the syntactic and semantic patterns of repetition make it fairly easy to detect the underlying paradigm. The essential paradigm of this discourse has the following structure:

1   What are these characteristic features which outstand in making the English language what it is, which give it its individuality and make it of this worldwide significance?

2   First and most important is its extraordinary receptive and adaptable heterogeneousness—the varied ease and readiness with which it has taken to itself material from almost everywhere in the world and has made the new elements of language its own.

3   A second outstanding characteristic of English is its simplicity of inflexion—the ease with which it indicates the relationships of words in a sentence with only the minimum of change in their shapes or variation of endings.

4   A third quality of English, therefore, is its relatively fixed word-order.

5   Another consequence, fourthly, of the loss of reduction to the minimum of the inflexions which English once had, is the growth of the use of periphrases or roundabout ways of saying things, and of the use of prepositions to take the place of the lost inflexions.

6   A fifth quality of English—though this, like the loss of inflexions and its consequences is shared with some other languages—is the development of new varieties of intonation to express shades of meaning which were formerly indicated by varying the shapes of words.

7   Not all the above qualities are in themselves necessarily good, nor have they all contributed to the general success of English.

8   But it seems probable that of them all it is the adaptable receptiveness and the simplicity of inflexion that have done most in this regard.

The purpose of this kind of analysis is not only to reveal the underlying principles that inform discourse, but also to make them generative (in the sense of actually producing discourse). The abstracted paradigm can be reindividuated in new content and can thus be used as the informing principle to generate new discourse. The informing principle of this discourse is logical analysis (more specifically, division into parts combined with enumeration). As a formal principle, it enables the mind to follow an analytical process and to experience new subject matter in a similar way.

In many instances, the simple procedure of abstracting the original sentences from the text is sufficient to reveal the underlying paradigm. Often, however, a slight normalization of the text is useful:

1 What are the outstanding characteristics of the English language that give it its individuality and make it of worldwide significance?

2 The first characteristic is the ease with which it has been able to assimilate new elements from other languages.

3 A second characteristic is its simplicity of inflexion.

4 A third characteristic is its relatively fixed word order.

5 A fourth characteristic is the growth in the use of periphrases and in the use of prepositions to replace the lost inflexions.

6 A fifth characteristic is the development of new varieties of intonation to express shades of meaning formerly indicated by varying the shapes of words.

7 Not all of these characteristics are necessarily good and not all have contributed to the general success of English, but it seems that of them all the adaptable receptiveness and the simplicity of inflexion have contributed the most.

This kind of normalization of the text has several advantages: First, it eliminates the redundancies and the irregularities in syntax of the original sentences. Second, it reveals the linguistic structure more clearly. Third, it illuminates more fully the underlying conceptual structure.

The regularity of syntax and the elimination of redundancies become apparent simply by comparing the "normalized" versions of these sentences with their originals. The basic syntactic pattern of the "core" sentences of the paradigm (sentences 2 through 6) is noun phrase–copula–noun phrase. Sentences 1 and 7 have a different linguistic form because they function differently in the discourse. These sentences constitute the introduction and the conclusion of the paradigm. The underlying conceptual structure is that of logical analysis. Two kinds of semantic clues lead us to a fuller understanding of this structure: the repetition of the word "characteristics" and the repetition of the ordinal numbers, first, second, third. The enumeration pattern gives added strength and emphasis to the analysis pattern.

Not every text, of course, has the same number of semantic or syntactic clues as this one. Not every text has the paragraphs arranged in such a convenient order. Some texts may have several introductory or concluding paragraphs as well as numerous transitional paragraphs which seem to be only remotely connected to the conceptual pattern. Nevertheless, with enough patience and skill in analyzing, we should be able to abstract the underlying paradigm by adding, deleting, and rearranging the basic elements.

Ideally, we would like to be able to abstract the essential paradigm from each kind of conceptual structure (analysis, comparison, classification) which constitutes a kind of prototype or archetype of the respective patterns. In some instances we can approach this ideal by analyzing and comparing enough texts, ignoring for the most part superficial or surface differences. But some conceptual structures seem to admit of a number of different paradigms (comparison and cause and effect, for example). Therefore, the task of the analyst is to describe as many of these conceptual patterns as possible.

For pedagogical purposes it might be useful to work with a number of essays which reveal structural affinities. In this way we can not only test the hypothesis that these conceptual patterns recur frequently in discourse, but we can also come nearer to approaching the essential paradigm.

The following discourse, taken from a section of a chapter in *The American Story*, entitled "The Frontier Disappears," supports the contention that many essays, despite surface differences, are related to each other on some deeper level of structure. A syntagmatic analysis discloses the following pattern:

THE FRONTIER DISAPPEARS

I

1 The United States of today is the product of a variety of forces: its European origins, the continuing impact of ideas from abroad, the constant mingling of peoples, and the changes wrought by the Industrial Revolution.

    2 Yet none of these forces was more significant than the frontier in endowing the Americans with the traits that distinguish them from other peoples of the world.

        3 Down to the present time many of our basic attitudes toward society and the world around us reflect that pioneer background.

2
4 What are the characteristics that are traceable to this unique feature of our inheritance?

3
5 We are a mobile people, constantly on the move, and but lightly bound to home or community.

   6 If you were to ask any group of Americans today how many live in the homes where they were born, or where their parents were born, only a handful would reply in the affirmative.

   6 If you asked that same question of a group of Englishmen or Frenchmen or Italians, an opposite answer would be given.

      7 Like our frontier ancestors, who shifted about so regularly that mobility became a habit, we are always ready for any change that promises to better our lives.

4
5 We are a wasteful people, unaccustomed to thrift or saving.

   6 The frontiersmen established that pattern, for nature's resources were so plentiful that no one could envisage their exhaustion.

      7 Within a few years of the first Virginia settlement, for example, pioneers burned down their houses when ready to move west; thus they were allowed to retrieve nails, and none gave thought to the priceless hardwoods that went up in smoke.

   6 As a people we still destroy much that others would save.

      7 I had this driven home to me when, during a year's residence in England, I received a letter from one of that nation's largest bank's, enclosed in a

second-hand envelope that had been readdressed to me.

    8 Such saving would be unthinkable in the United States, where even the most insignificant bank would never address a client save on elaborately engraved stationery, usually with the names of all twenty-eight vice presidents parading down one side of the page.

5

5 We are a practical, inventive people on whom the weight of tradition rests but lightly.

    6 In many lands of the world, people confronted with an unpleasant situation will quietly adjust themselves; in the United States, a man's first impulse is to change things for the better.

        7 This willingness to experiment came naturally to the pioneers who had no precedents on which to build.

            8 It has remained a trait of the industrial pioneers, whose ability to adapt and change has laid the basis for America's supremacy as a manufacturing nation.

6

5 We are individualistic people, deeply resentful of any intrusion into our affairs by government or society, also a basic attitude among frontiersmen.

    6 Aware that they were living in a land where resources were so abundant that only their own energies were necessary for success, they wanted to be left alone above all else.

        7 This trait persisted in American thought, even though the passing of

the frontier has forced the government to adopt a more positive social
role.

8 Even today such activity is
more resented in the United
States than elsewhere; and this
resentment also helps explain
the almost fanatical American
hatred of political systems such
as fascism or communism that
are based on the subjugation
of the individual.

7
5 We are a democratic people.

6 Our pioneering forefathers originated
neither the theory nor the practice of
democracy; the western world was well on
its way to political equalitarianism when
the continent was settled.

7 But conditions in frontier commu-
nities vastly stimulated the trend.

8 There nature reduced men to
equality by dimming the importance of wealth, or heredi-
tary privilege.

8 There poverty served as a great
leveler.

8 There the demand for self-rule
was particularly strong, for
frontiersmen knew that their
problems were unique and
must be solved locally.

9 And so on the frontier
the democratic tradition
was strengthened, until
it became a part of the
American creed.

10 The undying ha-
tred of the United
States for all forms
of totalitarianism

only mirrors the
strength of this
faith.

8

2 Thus has the frontier placed its stamp on America and its
people.
   3 In the continuing rebirth of civilization during the three
   centuries required to settle the continent, nature modified
   the characteristics of its conquerors, even in the midst of
   their conquest.
      4 There emerged a new people, robust and strong, with
      an unwavering faith in the merits of the individual
      and an unswerving allegiance to the principles of
      democracy.
         5 The frontier is no more, but its heritage remains
         to give a strength as well as individuality to the
         civilization of the United States.

A syntagmatic analysis is an essential first step in any kind of rhetorical analysis. This kind of analysis reveals that every discourse is
unique, that its subject matter, overall organization, paragraph structure,
sentence structure, and diction depend not only on formal considerations
but also on the author's purpose, his audience, his message, and so on.
A paradigmatic analysis, on the other hand, reveals that particular instances of discourse are related to each other by underlying principles.

The superficial structure of this discourse contrasts with that of the
previous discourse in significant ways: in content, organization, paragraph structure, sentence structure, sentence length, and so on. But the
underlying structures of both essays disclose structural affinities, as the
following analysis reveals:

   1 What are the characteristics that are traceable to this unique
   feature of our inheritance?

   2 We are a mobile people, constantly on the move, and but lightly
   bound to home or community.

   3 We are a wasteful people, unaccustomed to thrift or saving.

4   We are a practical, inventive people on whom the weight of tradition rests but lightly.

5   We are individualistic people, deeply resentful of any intrusion into our affairs by government or society, also a basic attitude among frontiersmen.

6   We are a democratic people.

7   Thus has the frontier placed its stamp on America and its people.

A slight normalization of the text results in the following schema:

1   What are the characteristics traceable to this unique feature of our inheritance?

2   We are a mobile people.

3   We are a wasteful people.

4   We are a practical, inventive people.

5   We are individualistic people.

6   We are a democratic people.

7   These are the characteristics that have enabled the frontier to place its stamp on America and its people.

The underlying pattern of this discourse is essentially the same as that of the previous discourse. Both paradigms are based on the conceptual structure of logical analysis. Both have an introductory sentence and a concluding sentence. The core sentences of each paradigm constitute the body of the paradigm; each gives a specific characteristic of the main idea. The semantic clues in the second paradigm, however, are not as numerous as in the first. The word "characteristics" appears only once in the discourse, in the fourth sentence of the text (sentence 1 of the paradigm). It is included in the last sentence of the paradigm to make the structure more apparent. (One could argue that it appears in the deep structure and that it gets into the surface structure by means of a transformation.) The text could undergo another kind of normalization, however, in which all of the sentences would include the key word (or one of its synonyms, such as "aspects," "features," "particles," "segments") in their basic structures. There are no semantic clues to indicate a subsidiary pattern of enumeration in the second paradigm.

Thus far, the models I have been working with have been relatively simple. For the most part, the simple procedure of abstracting the original sentences from the text has been sufficient to reveal the underlying paradigm. The following discourse, taken from *The Meaning of a Liberal Education,* by Everett Dean Martin, presents a slightly more difficult problem for analysis:

TYPES OF COLLEGE STUDENTS

I

1 The motives which lead people to seek college education divide the students into three types.
  2 First there are the few who love learning.
    3 The spirit which once caused groups of young men to follow Abelard or Erasmus still brings an occasional youth to college.
      4 Such students may need guidance, advice, and the fellowship of mature scholars.
        5 It is not necessary to force them to study, or offer them "snap courses," or cram them for examination.
        5 Much of the procedure and regulation—the regimentation common in institutions of learning—is unnecessary and harmful to them.
        5 Most of them would become educated persons even if they never saw a college classroom.

2

  2 A second type of student attends college and university in large numbers.
    3 The motive is preparation for a professional career.
      4 Many of the best students belong to this type.
        5 Whether in addition to their professional training they ever gain a liberal education—we have seen that the two are not necessarily the same—will depend largely on what they do after they get their degrees.
          6 If they then have an interest in educating themselves, their technical training ought

to be an advantage, for most of them have learned how to study.

7   But so much purely technical knowledge must be drilled into a man's head that the student who is preparing for a degree in engineering, law, medicine, or scientific research has very little time for anything else.

8   Many of the most successful physicians, engineers, and scientists need adult education quite as much as do ordinary working men.

3

2   The third type, the majority of undergraduate students, are for the most part pleasant young men and women of the upper middle class.

3   Their parents are "putting them through college" because it is the expected thing to do.

4   A man wishes to give his children every advantage.

5   While a bachelor's degree is not exactly a social necessity, there are many who would have something like an inferiority complex without it.

6   I knew one family in New York City who almost went into mourning when the only son failed in his Harvard entrance examinations.

4   Students of this type enjoy four happy years, largely at public expense, with other young people of their own age in an environment designed to keep them out of mischief.

5   I have no doubt this grown-up kindergarten life is good for them; most of them seem to appreciate it.

6   In later years they remain enthusiastically loyal to Alma Mater, coming back to football games and class reunions and contributing to the support of the college.

6   As alumni their influence is not always on the side of progress in education, but

perhaps they make-up for this failure in other ways.

As in the previous analyses, a syntagmatic analysis enables us to get at the underlying paradigmatic structure. In this discourse, however, in contrast to the previous examples of discourse, the organizational paradigm is not revealed by a simple sequence of isolated sentences, but by a cluster of such sentences as the following pattern indicates:

1. The motives which lead people to seek college education divide the students into three types.
2. First there are the few who love learning.
3. A second type of student attends college and university in large numbers. The motive is preparation for a professional career. Many of the best students belong to this type.
4. The third type, the majority of undergraduate students, are for the most part pleasant young men and women of the upper middle class. Their parents are "putting them through college" because it is the expected thing to do.

This paradigm presents a different problem from those of the previous paradigms. Not only must the sentences be paraphrased to eliminate the redundancies and the irregularities in meaning and syntax of the original sentences, but they must also be condensed to reveal the paradigmatic structure of the whole more clearly. As a preliminary step to making the paraphrase, we might regroup the meaning elements in the various sentences that make up the paradigm into semantic clusters:

first	there	are	the few	who love learning
a second	type	attends	large numbers many	motive is preparation for a professional career
				the best students
the third	type	are	the majority	parents are "putting them through college" because it is the expected thing to do

pleasant young men
and women of the up-
per middle class

This kind of regrouping of the elements into a semantic paradigm clearly reveals a number of things: the enumeration pattern ("first," "a second," "the third"), the main syntactic patterns (expletive–verb, subject–verb, subject–verb), the class terms ("the few," "large numbers," "many," "the majority"), and the differentiae ("who love learning," "motive is preparation for a professional career," "the best students," "parents are 'putting them through college' because it is the expected thing to do," "pleasant young men and women of the upper middle class"). The resultant para-phrase gives rise to the following paradigm:

1. The motives which lead people to seek college education divide the students into three types.

2. First there are the few who love learning.

3. A second type are the many, the large numbers, (usually) the best students, (whose) motive is preparation for a professional career.

4. The third type are the majority, pleasant young men and women of the upper middle class, (whose) parents are "putting them through college" because it is the expected thing to do.

The reasoning behind this particular form of paraphrase is that since the main meaning element of the classification pattern is carried by the nominal in sentence 2 ("the few who love learning"), it makes sense to put the subsequent semantic clusters in nominal form ("the many . . ." "the majority . . .").

The final step is to "normalize" the sentence structure by means of a condensed paraphrase, using what Doležel calls "a certain formal or semantic criterion of relevance," in order to eliminate redundancies and irregularities of syntax. The result is the following paradigm:

1. The motives which lead people to seek college education divide the students into *three types*.

2. The *first type* are *the few* who love learning.

3. The *second type* are *the many* whose motive is preparation for a professional career.

4. The *third type* are *the majority* whose parents are "putting them through college" because it is the expected thing to do.

Although the underlying structure of this discourse is that of a classification paradigm, it is similar in many respects to that of the analysis paradigm.

Pedagogical Application

For pedagogical purposes, we could abstract even more from the original paradigms, reducing the underlying pattern to a single abstract formula:

1. Introduction (includes main semantic clue)
2. Characteristic 1 (or Type 1)
3. Characteristic 2 (or Type 2)
4. Characteristic 3 (or Type 3)
5. Characteristic 4 (or Type 4)
6. Characteristic 5, 6, 7 . . . (or Types 5, 6, 7 . . .)
7. Conclusion (repeats main semantic clue)

The usefulness of paradigms in getting the novice student to produce competent writing may best be illustrated by a cursory examination of the following student essay, written in conscious imitation of a "process" paradigm:

HOW TO GET INTO TROUBLE

As we enter the 1970's, the goal of every college age American is to get into trouble. To many students, trouble has become a status symbol. Bruises received from policemen—pigs in the vernacular—are displayed with as much pride as the Congressional Medal of Honor. Unfortunately, only a small minority of students have the natural knack for getting into trouble, but the rest can be helped by an examination of the proper procedures.

First, select an appropriate official to get in trouble with. College presidents and deans are good because they are always available and near at hand. Mayors are adequate, especially in smaller cities where they have little to do and are particularly sensitive about it. Governors are often too remote. Consider, above all, the official's ability to get headlines. Anyone who can obtain publicity will do.

Second, raise an issue. It must be one in which the official is depicted as a neo-Nazi about to impose fascism on the nation. This requires only that he say no to a request to do something within his jurisdiction. If he has refused permission to stage a concert in the Municipal Stadium, or to bring a certain speaker to campus, or to make love in the Encanto Bandshell, he is the oppressor of human liberty and the Bill of Rights may be invoked against him.

Third, prepare a confrontation. Defiantly the official's edict is denounced, and plans are publicly proclaimed signaling the intent to go ahead with the prescribed act. Fierce rhetoric, threatening destruction to all opposition, is mandatory at this stage. It insures the presence of authorities to prevent said destruction. A confrontation with no one to confront, an ignominious possibility, is thus averted.

Fourth, confront. In accordance with announced plans, begin performance of the prescribed act. When the officials and authorities attempt to stop it, hurl at them invective and anything else within reach. Call liberals fascists. Call conservatives communists. The more effective they may be. Goad the authorities into forceful action.

The person who follows these four simple steps is certain to be rewarded with ample trouble. It will be on his record forever for all to see, his youthful cohorts and the more mature people who hold society together.

Although this essay is not outstanding, it is competent in many ways. It is original, witty, well organized, and easy to follow. The opening paragraph provides a suitable introduction and states the thesis clearly. Each of the next four paragraphs outlines a step in the process. The last paragraph concludes the essay by a simple pattern of a "return to the beginning."

The underlying paradigm provides the following pattern:

1. Unfortunately, only a small minority of students have the natural knack for getting into trouble, but the rest can be helped by an examination of the proper procedures.

2. First, select an appropriate official to get in trouble with.

3. Second, raise an issue.

4. Third, prepare a confrontation.

5. Fourth, confront.

6. The person who follows these four simple steps is certain to be rewarded with ample trouble.

Student writing which uses paradigms as models need not always be so simplistic. Quite often such paradigms can lead to more sophisticated student writing, as indicated by the following student essay:

ON VIETNAM

Like Ramsey Clark, I try not to be a "blamer"—i.e., one who must fix blame on others for everything. At this stage in the war, pinning the blame on any one particular person, party, or administration would not only be very hard to do, but pointless as well. I think that to discuss the war in Vietnam, we must ask several fundamental questions.

First, has our involvement in Vietnam been worth the cost? To this, I answer no.

Second, are we fighting for people worthy of American support? Again, I answer in the negative.

Finally, is it the interest of the United States to remain in Vietnam? Again, I think not.

Allow me to begin with question one: "Has our involvement in Vietnam been worth the cost?" Let's total up the cost, and see what we have paid. First and foremost, 50,000 American lives have been lost in the humid jungles of Indochina. In addition, three times that number have been maimed and seriously wounded in combat in Vietnam. Among the other "costs" of the war include a seemingly endless inflation which was both started and complicated by the war. One of the biggest prices this country is paying daily for the war is an increased disaffection with its young people. For many, the war has driven this nation's youth into foreign countries to avoid having to participate in what they consider to be an immoral war. I do not necessarily condone this conduct; I am merely reporting it. The additions of "hard-hat" and "hippie" to our vocabulary I can trace to the pro- and anti-Vietnam War factions. In summary, the war has extracted a tremendous toll in American lives, American casualties, and prisoners-of-war. It has almost wrecked our economy. It has turned the young against the old—and vice-versa. It has torn this country apart. I am reminded of what Abraham Lincoln said on the eve of the Civil War. "A house divided against itself cannot stand." Has the cost been worth it? I say no.

Secondly, for whom have we been expending so much money, and so many lives? Great believers in democracy, lovers of freedom? Hardly. The Thieu-Ky government is as much a lover of freedom and the democratic process as was Vice President Ky's personal hero, Adolph Hitler. Unfortunately, very few Americans are aware of a man named Zin, who ran against President Thieu in the last South Vietnamese election and lost. Unlike most candidates who lose in other countries, Zin's problems were not simply his election defeat. Because he ran a "coalition government" campaign (he ran as a peace candidate) Mr. Zin found himself in jail the day following the election.

One of the most shocking items to come from Thieu and Ky were the disclosures of their "Tiger cages" used for the suppressing of political opponents. I have been critical of the American prison system in other papers. But nothing in America is the rival of the tiger cage. I have not included a discussion of how Thieu and Ky do not permit magazines, notably particular issues of *Life, Time,* and *Newsweek,* into their country whenever a less-than-favorable article is included in the offending publication.

It seems to me that totalitarianism is bad—be it from the Communists (the Viet Cong) or from the Fascists (Thieu–Ky). Should the United States be a party to Thieu and Ky's dictatorship? I think not.

Finally, is the defense of South Vietnam either necessary or beneficial to the United States? Clearly, the answer is no. If, as some suggest, it is the duty of the U.S. to destroy Communism wherever it happens to be, why has our army gone thousands of miles to Vietnam when Cuba lies but 90 miles from our shores? I think that we can see that the so-called "Communist menace" is a sham. It simply won't hold water. What about the so-called "domino theory"? Again, this is a trick. If it is so likely that the Communists will take over other countries, why haven't the "dominos" done something in their *own* defense? What about Japan or Thailand? Why don't they send troops to "fight a war which should be fought by Asian boys"? Obviously, they don't view the threat as seriously as we seem to.

Considering the costs discussed above, I don't believe that there is any rational reason for saying that our Vietnam adventure is necessary, worth the costs, or morally right. For these reasons, I am against the war.

The underlying paradigm of this student essay is considerably more sophisticated than that of the previous essay as the following scheme indicates:

1. I think that to discuss the war in Vietnam we must ask several fundamental questions.

2. First, has our involvement in Vietnam been worth the cost?

3. Second, are we fighting for people worthy of American support?

4. Finally, is it in the interest of the United States to remain in Vietnam?

5. Allow me to begin with question one: "Has our involvement in Vietnam been worth the cost?"

6. Secondly, for whom have we been expending so much money and so many lives? Great believers in democracy, lovers of freedom?

7. Finally, is the defense of South Vietnam either necessary or beneficial to the United States?

8. Considering the costs discussed above, I don't believe that there is any rational reason for saying that our Vietnam adventure is necessary, worth the costs, or morally right.

The application of these principles to the study of rhetoric could become too mechanical and too formalistic unless the teacher emphasizes that a grasp of the underlying principles is more important than the abstract schema and the techniques used to analyze discourse. But at some stage in the writing process, the teacher can have no more important task than that of inculcating in the student a sense of form consciousness.

Structure in composition seldom exists for its own sake. It is, rather, an outward manifestation of an internal order. The mind, in the process of invention, creates orderly form. Because form in composition is so closely related to the process of invention which gives rise to form, conceptual structures in discourse must be conceived dynamically. These structures are not merely arrangements of static shapes. In the future, no rhetorician will be able to study the external forms of discourse without simultaneously studying their inner structures.

Notes

1. My discussion of paradigmatic analysis is based on the following texts: Lubomír Doležel, "Toward a Structural Theory of Content in Prose Fiction," in *Literary Style: A Symposium*, ed. Seymour Chatman (London and New York: Oxford University Press, 1971), pp. 95–110; William Oliver Hendricks, *Linguistics and the Structural Analysis of Literary Texts* (Ann Arbor: University Microfilms, Inc., 1969), pp. 76–125; Samuel R. Levin, *Linguistic Structures in Poetry* (The Hague: Mouton and Co., 1962); Claude Lévi-Strauss, "The Structural Study of Myth," in *Myth: A Symposium*, ed. Thomas A. Sebeok (Philadelphia: American Folklore Society, 1955), pp. 53–65; V. Propp, *Morphology of the Folktale*, 2nd ed. (Austin and London: University of Texas Press, 1968); Boris Tomashevsky, "Thematics," in *Russian Formalist Criticism*, trans. and with an Introduction by Lee T. Lemon and Marion J. Reis (Lincoln, Nebraska: University of Nebraska Press, 1965), pp. 61–95.

VII

STYLE AND STRUCTURE

His ideas are like Crawford + windows Piaget. [handwritten marginal note]

Thus far in our delineation of the conceptual theory of rhetoric, we have made three terms nearly synonymous: the topics of invention, the patterns of arrangement, and the characteristics of style. In classical rhetoric and in many traditional classroom approaches to style, style is seen as an embellishment of something more basic in discourse. It is something that one does with sentences after the inventive process takes place and after the ideas obtained through the process of invention are put into a formal pattern of arrangement. But, as Kenneth Burke points out, style (or eloquence, as he terms it) is not the mere embellishment of a more stable quality in discourse; it is its very essence, for the elements of formal appeal "are subtilized, carried down into the writing of a line or a sentence, until in all its smallest details, the work bristles with disclosures, contrasts, restatements with a difference, ellipses, images, aphorism, volume, sound values, in short all that complex wealth of minutiae which in their line-for-line aspect we call style and in their broader outlines we call form." [1] Thus style in the theory of conceptual rhetoric is inseparable from form except insofar as we elect to focus on aspects of form on the sentence level and designate these aspects as stylistic. Therefore, elements of structure such as definition, partition, exemplification, enumeration, cause and effect, contrast, metaphor, and the like can be found on the sentence level as well as on the discourse level and can accordingly be considered stylistic. This approach to style does not negate grammatical or rhetorical approaches. It seeks to isolate those features of style that may be termed "conceptual" and to relate them to formal patterns on varying levels of discourse.

Interestingly enough, the schemes and tropes of classical rhetoric are eminently suggestive of how certain aspects of formal appeal can be "subtilized" and "carried down into the writing of a line or a sentence." For example, on the sentence level, the stylistic devices of antithesis, antimetabole, chiasmus, and oxymoron can be considered stylistic variations of the formal principle of difference. Similarly, the stylistic devices of simile, metaphor, allusion, metonymy, synechdoche, and personification can be considered subtilized stylistic variations of the formal pattern of similarity. Formal patterns of arrangement on the paragraph level and on the discourse level obviously share structural characteristics with formal patterns of style on the sentence level.

As a way of envisioning the shared structural relationships that exist between sentences and longer units of discourse, let us consider the following tentative scheme:

Logical Elements of Style

I. Static Stylistic Elements
 A. Description
  1. Objective
  2. Impressionistic
 B. Definition
  1. Genus-species
  2. Etymology
  3. Synonym
 C. Division into Parts
  1. Partition
  2. Enumeration
   a. Seriation
   b. Asyndeton
   c. Polysyndeton
   d. Parallelism
 D. Classification
 E. Exemplification
 F. Comparison
  1. Similarity

        a. Literal
        b. Figurative
            1) Simile
            2) Metaphor
            3) Allusion
            4) Metonymy
            5) Synecdoche
            6) Personification
    2. Difference
        a. Kind
            1) Contrast
            2) Antithesis
            3) Antimetabole
            4) Chiasmus
            5) Oxymoron
        b. Degree
            1) Greater
            2) Lesser

II. Progressive Stylistic Elements
    A. Narration
    B. Process
    C. Cause and Effect
        1. Antecedent–consequent
        2. Reason–result
        3. Concession–assertion
    D. Syllogistic Progression
        1. Enthymeme

III. Repetitive Stylistic Elements
    A. Iteration
        1. Anaphora
        2. Epistrophe
        3. Epanalepsis
        4. Anadiplosis
        5. Antimetabole
        6. Polyptoton
        7. Epanodos
        8. Synonymia

B. Negation
C. Alternation

This scheme reveals a number of interesting things. The first is the extent to which elements of style can be related to elements of structure. Thus, for example, metaphor can be considered an aspect of style or an element of structure. (We can give a concise, one sentence metaphorical comparison of a person or a thing or we can use an extended metaphor consisting of a group of sentences.) Examples can be given in sentences or in longer units. The same is true of the other categories. The fact that we tend to think of some categories in relation to structure and some in relation to style is strictly a convention. The smaller elements we arbitrarily call style; the broader elements we arbitrarily call form or structure.

The second thing that this scheme reveals is the possibility of using figures of style for heuristic purposes. This idea simply confirms a point already made earlier that elements of style, when viewed as symbols of underlying thought processes, are "topical" and can thus be made to perform a heuristic function. Thus the wheel comes full circle: the elements of style, the patterns of arrangement, and the topics of invention are synonymous. How they are considered under these varying aspects depends upon ones point of view.

The nonlogical elements of style are much more difficult to deal with than the logical elements of style. Because the linguistic forms of nonlogical discourse are not arranged in logical patterns, the syntax is often dystaxic, and semantic stylistic features seem to take precedence over syntactic features. Rather than attempt to relate the nonlogical features of style to the nonlogical topics and patterns of arrangement, which are in themselves tentative and exploratory. I will list a few tentative examples below:[2]

Nonlogical Elements of Style

1. Neologisms
2. Parasemy
3. Polysemy
4. Homophones
5. Puns

6. Figurative language

7. Symbols

The making of neologisms (new words or expressions or the use of established words in new senses) can be a logical or a nonlogical process. The word "brunch," for instance, a combination of "breakfast" and "lunch" is a good example of a neologism which seems to have been consciously formed. Another example is the portmanteau word "chortle," a blending of "snort" and "chuckle," in Lewis Carroll's *Jabberwocky*. Neologisms are frequently found in dreams and in pathological language. Heinz Werner and Bernard Kaplan, in their discussion of the handling of linguistic forms in dreams, give the example of the word "peticularity," from a dream, which condensed the words "petty," "meticulous," and "regularity" into one form. Neologisms, then, are one kind of semantic stylistic element found in nonlogical discourse.

Parasemy is another kind of semantic feature found in nonlogical discourse. In parasemy, the meanings of the words are allusive, condensed, or elliptical. Werner and Kaplan relate that the idea "It would have broken the girl's heart if her boy friend had left her" was expressed in a dream as "the maid would fall (=break) into rods and sticks (=pieces)—it would be said that the fellow had gone up (=gone off)."

Polysemy, the use of multiple references and meanings which would be clearly differentiated on the conscious level, but condensed and less specific on the unconscious level, is a semantic element that is manifested in various ways in nonlogical discourse—in neologisms, in puns, and in double-entendres. These forms are used as much in everyday speech as they are in nonlogical discourse.

Homophones are words that are pronounced alike but that differ in meaning, derivation, or spelling. They are based on sound or "clang" relationships. In another dream quoted by Werner and Kaplan the word "senile" was pronounced by the dreamer almost like "snail" and connected to the word "sail" in the sentence, "Old age is not so bad; slow but quite smooth sailing in old age."

The main thing to remember about the stylistic features of nonlogical discourse is that the words are closely connected to images. This handling of words as if they were things is not only a feature of discourse such as dream speech, reveries, and schizophrenic speech, but as Vygotsky has pointed out, it is also a characteristic of the early speech of children.

Style as Structure

The idea of style as structure is one that conceives of style as the totality of an extended discourse. In this view, style is more than a string of isolated stylistic features that can be easily identified and classified on the sentence level. According to Michael Riffaterre, "a linguistic unit acquires, changes, or loses its stylistic effect according to position."[3] Context is of the utmost importance. Riffaterre continues, "If literary language is analyzed as a sequence of contexts, then proper emphasis will fall on the enrichment furnished by new stylistic possibilities."[4] Despite the apparent truth of these observations, however, I know of few linguistic or rhetorical studies which attempt to show the complex interrelationships that exist between style and structure. In order to illustrate the close relationship that exists between style and structure, I would like to analyze and comment upon the following prose passage from Thomas Wolfe's novel, *You Can't Go Home Again:*

Some things will never change. Some things will always be the same. Lean down your ear upon the earth, and listen.

The voice of forest water in the night, a woman's laughter in the dark, the clean, hard rattle of raked gravel, the cricketing stitch of midday in hot meadows, the delicate web of children's voices in bright air—these things will never change.

The glitter of sunlight on roughened water, the glory of the stars, the innocence of morning, the smell of the sea in harbors, the feathery blur and smoky buddings of young boughs, and something there that comes and goes and never can be captured, the thorn of spring, the sharp and tongueless cry—these things will always be the same.

All things belonging to the earth will never change—the leaf, the blade, the flower, the wind that cries and sleeps and wakes again, the trees whose stiff arms clash and tremble in the dark, and the dust of lovers long since buried in the earth—all things proceeding from the earth to seasons, all things that lapse and change and come again upon the earth—these things will always be the same, for they come up from the earth that never changes, they go back into the earth that lasts forever. Only the earth endures, but it endures forever.

The tarantula, the adder, and the asp will also never change. Pain and death will always be the same. But under the pavements trembling like a pulse, under the buildings trembling like a cry, under the waste of time, under the hoof of the beast above the broken bones of cities, there will be something growing like a flower, something bursting from the earth again, forever deathless, faithful, coming into life again like April.[5]

My examination will include the following:

1. a brief discussion of the rhetorical context of the passage;

2. a word for word tabulation of sentence length, paragraph length, and discourse length;

3. a sentence by sentence description of the potentially significant linguistic and rhetorical features within each sentence;

4. a description of the potentially significant features of relationships between each sentence and all of the preceding sentences;

5. a description of the structural features of the whole passage;

6. an interpretation of the passage, including an explanation of the linguistic and rhetorical features and the rhetorical method in terms of the interpretation; and

7. a summary of the generalizations implied about the conventions and devices of this kind of description.

The general approach to style derives from the contextual method for the description of prose style suggested by various commentators [6] and from my own limited work in contextual analysis.[7] The study of sentence length, paragraph length, and discourse length is derived from Edward P. J. Corbett's method of analyzing the style of Swift's *A Modest Proposal*.[8] The rhetorical analysis of sentences borrows from classical rhetoric. The method used to describe the sentence and intersentence relationships is based on a combination of a modified version of tagmemic analysis and Francis Christensen's approach to the rhetoric of the sentence.[9] Transformational grammar seems limited in describing linguistic relationships beyond the sentence level; structural grammar is limited to a succession of binary cuts. With tagmemic grammar, however, cuts can be made simultaneously on any level of structure. This is especially important in determining intersentence relationships because successive sentences, and parts of sentences, can be seen in such a way that reveals structural affinities between sentences. The analyst is not limited to a succession of binary cuts although occasionally he may find such cuts useful. Christensen's method of analysis is helpful because it allows us to separate the free modifiers in a particular sentence, indent them and number them to reveal their basic relationships, and depict them graphically in relation to the rest of the sentence, and, most importantly, to the patterning parts of successive sentences.

The method used to describe the structural features of the whole passage is based primarily on the work done by Francis Christensen with the rhetoric of the paragraph and on my own work with the rhetoric of the essay.[10] This work has been heavily influenced, however, by Zellig Harris's discourse analysis, Samuel Levin's analysis of linguistic structures in poetry, Alton Becker's tagmemic approach to paragraph analysis, Paul Rodgers' discourse-centered rhetoric of the paragraph, Michael Grady's conceptual rhetoric of the composition, Claude Lévi-Strauss's structural study of myth, William Hendricks's structural analysis of literary texts, V. Propp's analysis of folktales, Boris Tomashevsky's motif analysis, and Lubomir Doležel's structural study of content in prose fiction.[11] The kinds of analyses I feel are most useful for analyzing structural units larger than a paragraph are those illustrated in previous chapters, the syntagmatic and the paradigmatic.

Literary Context

The specific scene which supplies the context for the passage is late summer of 1929 in Manhattan. George Webber, the protagonist of the novel, has come back home to America after going to Europe to forget the woman he loved. Before he left Europe, he had become increasingly at odds with himself. The woman he loved was married; his behavior with her had been unpredictable and fanciful. They quarreled often, and he began to sense a growing madness within himself. Finally, he knew he must leave, not only because he felt he needed some time away from Esther, but also because he believed that he must learn for himself some of the truths of human existence. Each man, he believed, can only learn the lessons that life teaches by extracting them from his own experiences, be they true or false, foolish or profound. In Europe, George finds some of the things for which he had been searching, and when he returns home he is quieter and more predictable.

One evening he notices activity at the warehouse across the street from his front window. Drivers and packers come and go; helpers and handlers swarm all over the loading platform. In the midst of all this activity, George notices a man looking out into the street from a window in the warehouse. The man seems calm, immutable, unperturbed, impassive. As the men go about their tasks, he is scarcely aware of their existence. As George watches the scene, the man's face becomes for him "the symbol of a kind of permanence in the rush and sweep of chaos in the city, where all things come and go and pass and are soon forgotten." [12] The face becomes for him "the face of Darkness and of time. It never spoke, and yet it had a voice—a voice that seemed to have the whole earth in it . . . the voice of evening and of night." [13] The voice then seems to speak to George, but in such a way that it appears as if it is George himself who is speaking in a kind of interior monologue. Ostensibly it is "the voice of evening and of the night," but more accurately perhaps the passage represents a stream of consciousness illustration of the meeting of the man and the moment—the moment in time when the mind is in readiness to arrive at that most difficult of all perceptions, the perception of the obvious.

Sentence Analysis

Now that the passage has been placed in a larger context, a sentence by sentence description of the potentially significant features of each sentence can be made.

The opening sentence of the discourse is short and concise:

Some things / will never change.

This sentence contains five words, with a basic pattern of subject and verb. Conceptually, the sentence is a simple negative assertion that conveys a sense of the permanency of certain forms of earthly existence.

The second sentence is also very brief (seven words):

Some things / will always be / the same.

The basic pattern is subject–linking verb–complement. In contrast to the opening negative assertion, this sentence restates the idea of the initial sentence in positive terms ("always be the same").

The third sentence (nine words) is slightly longer than the two preceding:

Lean down / your ear / upon the earth, and listen.

This sentence contains two main clauses. The first consists of the main verb plus particle ("lean down"), and a noun phrase object ("your ear"). The basic pattern is extended by the prepositional phrase "upon the earth." The second clause consists of the single verb "listen." The placement of the two verbs in parallel structure together with the alliteration of their initial /l/ sounds creates syntactical and rhythmical balance.

Sentence 4 is the only sentence in the second paragraph:

2 The voice of forest water in the night,   (NP)
2 a woman's laughter in the dark,   (NP)
2 the clean, hard rattle of raked gravel,   (NP)
2 the cricketing stitch of midday in hot meadows,   (NP)
2 the delicate web of children's voices in bright air—   (NP)
1 these things / will never change.

This sentence contains 43 words. It uses a cataloging technique to present specific examples of the recurrent, permanent things of the earth. The basic sentence pattern is subject–verb (level 1). The conceptual structure is negative assertion. The base is expanded by a series of front-shifted noun phrases that present specific examples of things of the earth that will never change. Rhetorically, the sentence contains elements of the periodic sentence and of parallelism. The base clause follows a series of parallel phrases, repeats the idea they contain in more general terms, and acts as a summary statement for the particulars. In this way the meaning unfolds gradually until it reaches the main idea at the end of the sentence. Each appositive noun phrase contains a single sensory image: the sound of flowing water, the sound of a woman's laughter, the sound of raked gravel, the cricketing sound of midday, and the sound of children's voices. In addition to these semantic "sense" clusters, there is a negative–positive movement carried by the prepositional phrases: night/midday, dark/bright. There is also a pattern of alternation between the human and the nonhuman (water/woman, crickets/children) as well as a pattern of movement from adulthood (close to death) to childhood (close to birth). Thus structural alternation appears at different levels of semantic organization. Finally, each of the images isolates a moment in process.

Rhythm and sound devices contribute to the expressiveness of the sentence. The most obvious source of rhythm is the periodic structure. The long series of parallel noun phrases within the periodic structure develops a rhythmic momentum until its culmination in the main clause at the end of the sentence. Another source of the rhythm is the repetition of determiners in the initial positions of their respective phrases.

The repetition of sound patterns is another stylistic feature. For example, in the phrase, "the *v*oi*c*e of the *f*ore*st* water in the night," soft, fricative sounds suggest the sound of flowing water, while in the phrase "the *c*lean, har*d* ra*tt*le of ra*k*ed *g*ravel," hard consonant sounds suggest the sound of raked gravel.

The third sentence contains a single sentence similar in style to the previous one:

> 2 The glitter of sunlight on roughened water,   (NP)
> 2 the glory of the stars,   (NP)
> 2 the innocence of morning,   (NP)
> 2 the smell of the sea in harbors,   (NP)
> 2 the feathery blur and smoky buddings of young boughs,   (NP) and
> 2 something there that comes and goes and never can be captured,   (NP)
>   3 the thorn of spring,   (NP)
>   3 the sharp and tongueless cry,   (NP)
> 1 these things / will always be / the same.

This sentence contains sixty words. It uses a cataloging technique to enumerate the details of a long series of sensory images. Grammatically, the sentence has a basic pattern of subject–linking verb–complement (level 1) that is expanded by a series of noun phrases (levels 2 and 3). Rhetorically, it contains features of the periodic sentence and of parallel structure. Each noun phrase is arranged in balanced, parallel structure, and as the series advances the parallelism develops a rhythmic momentum and orders the particular details of the description until the generally stated summary idea is reached at the end of the sentence. The main idea, because it is delayed until the end, receives emphasis, and the parallelism, combined with the periodic structure, helps to create rhythm. Conceptually, the sentence is a positive assertion.

As in the previous sentence, the front-shifted appositives contain semantic "sense" clusters which are particular examples of the unchanging features of earthly existence: "the glitter of sunlight," "roughened water," "the smell of the sea," "the feathery blur and smoky buddings of young boughs." A few of the clusters are impressionistic and evocative: "the glory of the stars," "the innocence of morning," "the sharp and tongueless cry." Each appositive is a single image which isolates a moment in time. Another stylistic feature is semantic alternation: comes / goes, never / always.

Repetition is used at various structural levels. At the highest level there is repetition of similar grammatical patterns (8 noun phrases arranged in parallel structure). On the next level there is repetition of words at the beginning of the successive noun phrases (the anaphoric repetition of the determiner "the"). Finally, on the level of sound, the repetition of initial consonant sounds is found between phrases ("the glitter of sunlight on roughened water, the glory of stars"), and within phrases ("the smell of the sea in harbors, the feathery blur and smoky buddings of young boughs," and "something there that comes and goes and never can be captured").

Paragraph four (4) contains two sentences. The first sentence consists of 92 words:

1 All things belonging to the earth / will never change—
  2 the leaf,   (NP)
  2 the blade,   (NP)
  2 the flower,   (NP)
  2 the wind that cries and sleeps and wakes again,   (NP)
  2 the trees whose stiff arms clash and tremble in the dark, (NP) and
  2 the dust of lovers long since buried in the earth—   (NP)
  2 all things proceeding from the earth to seasons,   (NP)
  2 all things that lapse and change and come again upon the earth—   (NP)
1 these things / will always be / the same,
  2 for they come from the earth that never changes,   (SC)
  2 they go back into the earth that lasts forever.   (SC)

The first main clause (level 1) is a negative assertion; the second (the second level 1) is a positive assertion. The sentence contains two main clauses and two subordinate clauses. The first main clause ("All things belonging to the earth will never change") has a subject–verb pattern (things . . . will . . . change). It is expanded by a long series of back shifted appositive noun phrases. Each of these enumerates specific examples of the recurrent things of earthly existence. The second main clause ("these things will always be the same") contains a basic pattern of subject–linking verb–complement (things . . . will be . . . same). This clause acts as a summary statement for the long series of noun phrases and organizes the subordinate clauses ("for they come up from the earth that never changes, they go back into the earth that lasts forever") which follow. Each of these clauses has a basic pattern of subject–verb–particle ("they come up," "they go back"). Finally, within each of the subordinate clauses are clauses which contain an identical subject–verb pattern ("that changes," "that lasts forever").

The arrangement of clauses and phrases in parallel structure is another stylistic feature:

All things belonging to the earth will never change . . .
all things proceeding from the earth to seasons,
all things that lapse and change and come again upon the earth—
these things will always be the same. . . .

The balance in these lines is achieved by the repetition of similar syntactic structures, by the repetition of identical and near identical word groups at the beginning of the parallel structures, and by the use of approximately equal line lengths.

The series of noun phrases beginning with "the leaf" and ending with "the dust of lovers long since buried in the earth" are also arranged in parallel structure. Each contains a single image which particularizes the general idea of the first main clause. The first three noun phrases, "the leaf, the blade, the flower," are perfectly balanced by length. The next three phrases, "the wind that cries and sleeps and wakes again," "the trees whose stiff arms clash and tremble in the dark," and "the dust of lovers long since buried in the earth," are also balanced. Each contains a single image and each is of approximately the same length. The parallel structure helps to order the images and to emphasize them. It is also a source of prose rhythm.

Another type of parallel structure is antithesis. The contrast produced

by the antithesis of the clauses in the last two sentence levels ("they come
up from the earth that never changes, they go back into the earth that
lasts forever") points to the underlying paradox of one of the key ideas,
that of unchanging change. The things of the earth come forth, develop,
change, die, and come again, and therefore are a part of the permanent
and unchanging cycle of growth, death, and rebirth.

Polysyndeton is used to achieve emphasis and rhythmic variation.
Thus in the lines, "the wind that cries and sleeps and wakes again" and
"all things that lapse and change and come again upon the earth," the
regular accenting of the words and the emphasis on the ideas they
represent create a distinctive rhythm and suggest the endless cycle of
death and rebirth, thus reinforcing the theme.

The most obvious stylistic feature is repetition. On the highest
structural level, there is repetition of similar syntactic patterns:

they come up from the earth that never changes
they go back into the earth that lasts forever
All things belonging to the earth
all things proceeding from the earth
the wind that cries and sleeps and wakes again
all things that lapse and change and come again
the leaf
the blade
the flower

On the next level there is repetition of identical words and word groups.
The phrase "the earth" is repeated six times, the word "change," three
times, "never," twice, "come," twice, and the word "again," twice. The
phrase "all things" is stated at the beginning of line 1, repeated anaphor-
ically in lines 8 and 9, and then repeated in slightly varied form in line 10.
The determiner "the," because of its position at the beginning of a succession of noun phrases, has the force of anaphoric repetition in lines 2
through 7; similarly, the word "they" in lines 11 and 12. The following
scheme makes the repetition clearer:

1 *All things* belonging to *the earth*
                        will *never change—*
2   *the* leaf,
3   *the* blade,

4   *the* flower,
5   *the* wind that cries and sleeps and wakes *again,*
6   *the* trees whose stiff arms clash and tremble in
                the dark, and
7   *the* dust of lovers long since buried in *the earth*—
8 *all things* proceeding from *the earth* to seasons,
9 *all things* that lapse and *change* and *come again* upon *the earth*—
10 these *things*
                      will always be the same,
11   for *they come* up from *the earth*
                that *never changes,*
           they go back into *the earth*
                that lasts forever.

The repetition does a number of things: it creates an inescapable means of transition as each repetition occurs, it produces emphasis for key ideas, and it creates a distinctive rhythm.

This graphic depiction of structure brings out other distinctive stylistic features. There is a negative-positive pattern of alternation: never change / always be the same, never changes / lasts forever. There are patterns of contrast, occurrence and recurrence: sleeps / wakes, lapse / come again, come up from the earth / go back into the earth. In addition, there is a kind of organic progression: "leaf, blade, flower, tree" and "proceeding from the earth to seasons." And finally there are semantic "sense" clusters embedded in the noun phrase series: "the leaf, the blade, the flower, the wind that cries and sleeps and wakes again," and so forth.

The last sentence in paragraph 4 contains eight words:

Only the earth / endures,
but it / endures forever.

It consists of two short clauses in parallel structure. Each contains a subject–verb pattern. Each is similar in syntactic structure, length, and idea. Rhetorically, the sentence is balanced.

Other stylistic features include semantic alternation (only / but), repetition (endures . . . endures), and substitution (the earth . . . it). These stylistic features create emphasis and add to the rhythmic effect of the sentence.

The first sentence of the last paragraph has eleven words:

The tarantula, the adder, and the asp/
will also never change.

It has a pattern of three conjoined subjects and a verb. The rhetorical pattern is that of the three-part series ("the tarantula, the adder, and the asp"). The three-part series, not being unusually long, represents the norm. Many examples of things that cause pain and death could have been given, but these three examples are representative. The sentence also achieves a kind of syntactic and rhythmic balance, with the subject balanced against the predicate, and with each part receiving three major stresses. Vowel alliteration and assonance also enhance the rhythmic effect and help tie the series together ("the tarantula, the adder, and the asp").
The second sentence in this paragraph is slightly shorter:

Pain and death / will always be the same.

The basic pattern is subject–linking verb–complement. Rhetorically, the sentence contains a two-part series ("pain and death") which functions as the subject. The sentence achieves a kind of syntactic balance, with the subject balanced against the predicate.
The last sentence in this paragraph, and in the discourse, is one of the longest (fifty-five words) in the selection:

2   But under the pavements trembling like a pulse, (PP)
2   under the buildings trembling like a cry, (PP)
2   under the waste of time, (PP)
2   under the hoof of the beast above the broken bones
    of cities, (PP)
1   there / will be / something growing like a flower,
               / something bursting from the earth again,
2   forever deathless, (AC)
2   faithful, (Adj)
2   coming into life again like April. (VP)

The basic pattern is expletive–linking verb–noun, with the linking verb completed by a delayed conjoined subject ("something growing like a flower, something bursting from the earth again"). The sentence is characterized by a series of front-shifted and back-shifted free modifiers.
Rhetorically, the sentence is a periodic sentence, containing features

of the balanced sentence. The sentence begins with a series of introductory prepositional phrases which gradually build toward the main idea. The main idea is then partially stated by the sentence base (level 1). But because of the expletive–linking verb–noun construction, the subjects are delayed, and then because of the subsequent qualification of the subjects by modification, the main idea is not completed until the end of the sentence. The long series of opening phrases, because they are grammatically parallel and are of approximately the same length, begin to develop a semantic and syntactic rhythm momentum. Then the base interrupts momentarily, but its expansion by a sequence of balanced structures urges the sentence on to new parallels, each subsequent addition driving the movement downward until the main idea is finally concluded.

Semantically there are patterns of alternation and progression suggesting a movement from death to rebirth. The pattern of alternation is carried by a series of balanced prepositional phrases: "under the hoof of the beast/above the broken bones of cities." Patterns of progression are carried by a series of participial phrases: "trembling like a pulse," "trembling like a cry," "growing like a flower," "bursting from the earth again," "coming into life again like April." There is also a movement from negative semantic clusters to positive clusters: "the waste of time," "the hoof of the beast," "the broken bones of cities"; "something growing like a flower," "something bursting from the earth again," "forever deathless," "faithful," "coming into life again like April."

The repetition of similar syntactic patterns is an important stylistic feature. The repetition of parallel prepositional phrases:

under the pavements trembling like a pulse,
under the buildings trembling like a cry,
under the waste of time,
under the hoof of the beast above the broken bones of cities

The repetition of noun phrases:

something growing like a flower,
something bursting from the earth again

And within these larger syntactical structures, the repetition of participial phrases:

trembling like a pulse
trembling like a cry
growing like a flower
bursting like a flower
coming into life again like April

And finally, embedded in the participial phrases, these prepositional phrases:

like a pulse
like a cry
like a flower
like April
from the earth again
into life again

Another kind of repetition is of identical words. The repetition of the word "under" in the initial position is anaphoric. Other repeated words are "trembling" (repeated twice), and "like" (four times). On a lower level of structural organization there is repetition of the suffix "ing" in the sequence of present participles: "trembl*ing*," "grow*ing*," "burst*ing*," "com*ing*." The repetition does a number of things: it affords a means of transition within word groups and between word groups, it creates emphasis, it produces a distinctive rhythm, and it gives an almost rhyming effect to the lines. A slight realignment of the lines, together with the underlining of the key elements, makes the pattern more obvious:

But *under* the pavements
            trembling like a pulse
    under the buildings
            trembling like a cry,
    under the waste of time,
    under the hoof of the beast above the broken bones
    of cities,
there will be *something*
            growing like a flower
    something
            bursting from the earth *again,*
                forever deathless,

faithful,
coming into life *again* *like* April.

Intersentence Relationships

In the analysis of sentences so far, I have attempted to describe the relevant features of style and meaning within the individual sentence. However, the formal appeal of the sentence can also be determined by its place in a linguistic context. There are certain characteristics of style and meaning which seem to transcend the sentence level, and as soon as we begin to juxtapose any two sentences, we begin to see features which are not as apparent when we examine the sentences individually. The context seems to add to, diminish, or change the stylistic effect of the individual sentences. The contextual pattern permits the perception of similarities and contrasts, and of structural and semantic relationships. Any two successive sentences may be said to be in context with relationship to one another. A contextual analysis consists of dividing the respective sentences into their constituent parts and then showing the relationship of these parts to each other by matching the parts of one sentence against those of another.

Let us begin the contextual analysis by looking closely at the first two sentences of the discourse:

Some things / will never change
Some things / will always be the same.

The most obvious features revealed by this juxtaposition are those of repetition and variation. On the sentence level, the two sentences are parallel. The repetition of identical structures at the beginning of each sentence is the major source of similarity. The noun phrase subjects are repeated ("some things"), as are the auxiliaries ("will"). The parallel openers achieve emphasis by their position and by their repetition, and develop a distinctive rhythmic pattern.

The fact that the entire first sentence is a negative assertion and the second sentence restates the same idea in positive terms provides the major instance of variation. Between the two sentences the adverbials carry the chief contrast: never / always. But the contrast is also carried by a part of the verb phrase: change / be the same. Thus the opening pair of sentences seems to provide two major structural principles: repetition and negative-positive alternation. Both of these sentences are characterized by extreme brevity (five words, seven words). Therefore the sentences are related by length as well as by structure.

Sentence 3, the last sentence in the opening paragraph, seems to be an interruption, a departure from the structural features noted in the first two sentences:

Some things / will never change.
Some things / will always be the same.
Lean down / your ear upon the earth and listen.

The most radical change is that between the declarative mode of the first two sentences and the imperative mode of the third. Another difference is in the grammatical structure. When we next consider these sentences as a paragraph unit, we find that the first two sentences are coordinate. There is almost a point by point parallel relationship between the syntactic components. Semantically the second sentence is a positive restatement of the first. The third sentence, however, seems to share no structural relationship with the first two. This leads us to believe that the relationship of the sentences as a discrete paragraph is not important. Perhaps some larger structural principle is in operation. Also there is no discernible logical, chronological, or spatial principle at work in the paragraph to organize it as a paragraph. There is a lexical tie-in between the first two sentences. The repetition of identical words ("some things") in the first two sentences provides the means of transition. But the tie-in between the second and third sentences is very tenuous, suggesting that at best there is a meaning relationship which is understood. The parallel structure of the verbs in the third sentence suggests that the second parallel verb needs to be completed by a complement just as the first verb is. The sentence, with the implied element included in parentheses, might then be understood as follows: "Lean down your ear upon the earth, and listen" (to the things that will never change). Thus the sentences can be said to be related, but not in the way textbook explanations say that paragraphs should be related. Why then are these three sentences grouped together as a single paragraph? It may be that their function is more in keeping with the whole discourse than with a discrete segment of the whole. We might state provisionally that the function of these three sentences is to get the discourse going, to provide the initial impetus for the organization of the whole. Finally, we might note that there is a progressive lengthening in these sentences, from five words, to seven words, to nine words.

The next sentence in the discourse, sentence 4, is a complete paragraph. Its relationship to the previous sentence can be graphically depicted as follows:

Lean down / your ear upon the earth, and
listen.
    The voice of forest water in the night,
    a woman's laughter in the dark,
    the clean, hard rattle of raked gravel,
    the cricketing stitch of midday in hot meadows,
    the delicate web of children's voices in bright air—
these things / will never change.

When we view sentence 4 in the context of sentence 3, we find that the previous sentence, ending as it does with the verb "listen," seems to be incomplete. Because the clauses of the sentence are arranged in parallel structure and because the first main verb takes a direct object, we come to expect the second verb to be completed by an object. The form of the sentence, therefore, arouses in us a need for grammatical closure. "Lean down your ear upon the earth and listen," we are admonished. And as if in anticipation, we seem to answer, "Listen to what?" Then we are presented with a sequence of phrases in parallel order which enumerate the answer: "The voice of forest water in the night, a woman's laughter in the dark, the clean, hard rattle of raked gravel, the cricketing stitch of midday in hot meadows, the delicate web of children's voices in bright air." This sequence of images completes the idea contained in the previous sentence, and therefore we are gratified and fulfilled by the completed sequence. We seem to sense its logical and psychological rightness. Thus the very form of this sentence, with its periodic structure and its series of front-shifted parallel phrases, seems to be a "natural" consequence of its relative position in the discourse.

The length of the fourth sentence in relation to sentence 3 is striking. Sentence 4 contains forty-three words; sentence 3 contains nine words. The fourth sentence enumerates a lengthy series of images illustrating the sounds of the earth. This long series has been set up by the previous sentence so that the relationship between these two sentences almost seems to determine the sentence length of the fourth sentence. Sentence 4 also represents a progressive lengthening of successive sentences, a pattern initiated in the opening sentence.

If we view the fourth sentence in relationship to the previous sentences in paragraph 1, we find the following relationships: First, a part of the subject phrase ("things") of the first two sentences is repeated in the fourth sentence. Second, all of the verb phrase from sentence 1 ("will never change") is repeated in sentence 4. Variations include the substitution of the word "these" in the fourth sentence for the word "some" in the first two sentences. Also, the addition of the front-shifted appositives in sentence 4 varies the simple sentence pattern of the first two sentences.

Since the second paragraph consists of a single sentence, not much can be said in terms of contrasting the first and second paragraphs. The first paragraph consists of three short sentences containing twenty-one words. The second paragraph consists of a single long sentence of forty-three words. There is thus a progressive lengthening of paragraph length as well as of sentence length.

The fifth sentence is similar to sentence 4. Sentence 5 constitutes the entire third paragraph, sentence 4, the entire second paragraph. Both are long, with similar syntactic structures:

> The voice of forest water in the night,
> a woman's laughter in the dark,
> the clean, hard rattle of raked gravel,
> the cricketing stitch of midday in hot meadows,
> the delicate web of children's voices in bright air—
> these things / will never change.

> The glitter of sunlight on roughened water,
> the glory of the stars,
> the innocence of morning,
> the smell of the sea in harbors,
> the feathery blur and smoky buddings of young boughs, and
> something there that comes and goes and never can be
> captured,
> the thorn of spring,
> the sharp and tongueless cry—
> these things / will always be the same.

On the highest structural level, these two sentences are parallel. Both are periodic sentences. Both begin with a long series of coordinate noun phrases, and both conclude with similar sentence bases. On a lower level, the front shifted noun phrases are not only parallel to each other within their respective sentences, but they repeat this parallelism from sentence to sentence. Besides these patterns of repetition, on an even lower level the identical noun phrase subjects are repeated in the successive sentences ("these things"), and so are the auxiliaries ("will"). There are also patterns of alternation. For one thing, the entire sentence base in the fifth sentence is a positive alternation of the base in the fourth sentence: "these things will never change / these things will always be the same." The adverbials carry the main contrast: never / always. Then the last part of the verb phrase repeats the contrast: change / be the same. Thus the patterns of structural parallelism, repetition, and positive-negative alternation appear at different levels of linguistic organization in the discourse.

Sentence length continues to show a progression from the five words of the opening sentence to the seven, nine, and forty-three words respectively of the second, third, and fourth sentences, to the sixty words in this sentence. Paragraph length displays the same progression from twenty-one words (paragraph 1), to forty-three words (paragraph 2), to sixty words (in this paragraph).

The relationships between sentence 5 in the third paragraph and the sentences of the first paragraph are similar to those between sentence 4 and the same sentences. Sentence 5 repeats the structural parallelism of the second sentence ("some things will always be the same") just as sentence 4 repeats the structural pattern of the first sentence ("some things will never change," "these things will never change"). The subject phrase "things" is repeated, and all of the verb phrase is repeated. The word "these," however, is a variation on the pattern, substituting for the word "some." The addition of front shifted noun phrases also is a variation on the simple subject–verb pattern of the opening sentences.

Sentence 6, the first sentence in the fourth paragraph, presents an interesting contrast to sentence 5:

> The glitter of sunlight on roughened water,
> the glory of the stars,
> the innocence of morning,
> the smell of the sea in harbors,
> the feathery blur and smoky buddings of young boughs, and

something there that comes and goes and never can be captured,
the thorn of spring,
the sharp and tongueless cry—
these things / will always be the same.

All things belonging to the earth / will never change—
the leaf,
the blade,
the flower,
the wind that cries and sleeps and wakes again,
the trees whose stiff arms clash and tremble in the dark, and
the dust of lovers long since buried in the earth—
all things proceeding from the earth to seasons,
all things that lapse and change and come again upon the
earth—
these things / will always be the same,
for they come up from the earth that never changes,
they go back into the earth that lasts forever.

When we consider sentence 6 in the context of sentence 5 and of the previous sentences, a number of significant differences begin to emerge. The solemn, rigid order established by the sentences in the first three paragraphs is disheveled by the unruly rush of clauses and phrases in sentence 6, where the repeated elements are all mixed up. Clauses alternate with phrases, the appositive noun phrases which were front-shifted in sentences 4 and 5 are now back-shifted and buried, and identical repeated word groups which appeared in base clauses now alternate from clauses to phrases.

Some of the structural patterns, of course, are repeated from one sentence to another, but there are many variations on these patterns. On the highest structural level, the second base clause in sentence 6 ("these things will always be the same") is an exact repetition of the base clause in sentence 5. On the next level, the noun phrase series repeats the parallel structure of the appositive phrases in the previous sentence, but in sentence 5 the appositives are front-shifted, whereas in sentence 6 they are back-shifted. Also the first three appositives in the series in sentence 6 are unusually brief in comparison with those within the same sentence and in previous sentences.

The pattern of polysyndeton, carried by the dependent clauses, is repeated in sentence 6. Sentence 5 initiates the pattern and then sentence 6 picks it up twice:

> That comes and goes and never can be captured
> that cries and sleeps and wakes again
> that lapse and change and come again upon the earth

Other patterns of repetition include the following: a part of the subject noun phrase ("things") in the base clause of sentence 5 is repeated in sentence 6 in the first main clause; the entire subject noun phrase ("these things") of sentence 5 is repeated in the second main clause of sentence 6; the auxiliary "will" is repeated in all of the main or base clauses in sentences 5 and 6; finally, the entire verb phrase ("will always be the same") of the fifth sentence is repeated in the second base clause of the sixth sentence.

There are a number of variations on the repetition of words and phrases from sentence 5 to sentence 6. Some patterns are repeated in clauses, some are repeated in phrases, and some alternate between clauses and phrases. For example, the word "thing" is initiated as part of the compound word "something" in the front shifted appositive phrase in sentence 5, and repeated as a separate word in the main clause. Then it is picked up again in the opening main clause of sentence 6, repeated in two successive appositive phrases, and then repeated in the last main clause. Each time it is repeated it is part of a larger pattern which itself is repeated and then varied. The variations in turn, because they are repeated, form new patterns of repetition. Thus the noun phrase "these things," a variation of the phrase "some things" and the compound "something," forms a new pattern of repetition. Similarly the noun phrase "all things" is a variation on the previously stated noun phrases "some things" and "these things." The following scheme illustrates these variations:

> *something* there that comes and goes and never can be captured
> *these things* will always be the same
> *all things* belonging to the earth will never change
> *all things* proceeding from the earth to seasons
> *all things* that lapse and change and come again upon the earth
> *these things* will always be the same

In addition to the patterns of repetition, there are a number of patterns of alternation on various structural levels. On the clause level, the first main clause of the sixth sentence is a negative alternative to the positive statement of the base clause in sentence 5. The second main clause in sentence 6 is a positive alternating statement of the first main clause of the same sentence. The resultant alternating pattern may be depicted as follows:

these things will always be the same
all things . . . will never change
these things will always be the same

On a lower structural level, the following patterns of alternation are embedded in the verb phrases:

comes and goes and never can be captured
always be the same
never change
cries and sleeps and wakes again
lapse and change and come again
always be the same
come up
never changes
go back
lasts forever

One contrasting pattern is carried by the adverbials: never / always / never / again; again; always / never / forever. Verbs and participles provide another contrasting pattern: comes / goes / come, come up / go back. And finally some main verbs alternate with linking verb–complement patterns to produce the following contrasts: be the same / change / lapse / change / be the same / changes / lasts.

Progression in sentence and paragraph length seems to be a constant feature. The progression in sentence length from the opening sentence to the sixth sentence is as follows: five words, seven words, nine words, forty-three words, sixty words, and ninety-two words. Paragraph length varies from twenty-one words, to forty-three words, to sixty words, to one hundred words.

The contrast between sentence 7, the last sentence of the fourth paragraph, and sentence 6, the first sentence of this paragraph, is striking:

All things belonging to the earth / will never change—
    the leaf,
    the blade,
    the flower,
    the wind that cries and sleeps and wakes again,
    the trees whose stiff arms clash and tremble in the dark, and
    the dust of lovers long since buried in the earth—
    all things proceeding from the earth to seasons,
    all things that lapse and change and come again upon the
    earth—
these things / will always be the same,
    for they come up from the earth that never changes,
    they go back into the earth that lasts forever.

Only the earth / endures,
but it / endures forever.

The most manifest contrast is in sentence length. Up to this point, the sentences have been getting progressively longer. Sentence 7 is short and abrupt in comparison to sentence 6. Sentence 6 contains ninety-two words; sentence 7 contains eight words. Structurally sentence 7 consists of two short clauses of equal length. Sentence 6 also has two main clauses, but in addition, it contains a long series of back-shifted appositive noun phrases and a number of dependent clauses. Sentence 7, coming as it does at this point in the passage, interrupts a sequence of long sentences (4, 5, and 6) containing long strings of front-shifted and back-shifted appositive noun phrases.

The patterns which sentences 6 and 7 have in common include structural parallelism and semantic alternation. The two main clauses of sentence 7 are parallel to those of sentence 6:

All things belonging to the earth will never change. . . .
These things will always be the same. . . .
Only the earth endures,
but it endures forever.

On a lower organizational level, there are structural and semantic patterns of alternation and repetition. There are adverbial contrasts: never /

forever, always / only; and main verb contrasts: change / endures. The patterns of repetition include identical word and phrase repetition: the earth, forever; and semantic repetition: lasts, endures. These patterns of alternation and repetition advance the overall movement of alternation and repetition in the discourse as a whole.

Although sentences 6 and 7 constitute a complete paragraph, the sentences seem to be more important as elements in a larger structural organization than they do as a discrete paragraph. The repetition of the noun phrase "the earth" provides an explicit lexical tie-in between 6 and 7. But there is no distinctive paragraph movement as such.

Sentence 8 is the first sentence in the last paragraph. Its relationship to sentence 7 can be illustrated as follows:

Only the earth / endures,
but it / endures forever.

the tarantula, the adder and the asp /
will also never change.

Sentence 8 continues the pattern of negative–positive alternation between sentences. As in previous sentences, the adverbials carry the main contrast: only / forever / never. The main verbs also contribute to the pattern of alternation: endures / changes. These semantic contrasts are also the means by which the transition is made from paragraph 4 to paragraph 5.

Sentence 8 may also be related to sentence 6 in the previous paragraph. The main clause of sentence 8 is parallel to the main clauses of sentence 6:

All things belonging to the earth will never change . . .
these things will always be the same. . . .
the tarantula, the adder, and the asp will also never
change.

These clauses further the larger pattern of negative–positive alternation. The adverbials carry the main contrast: never / always / never. Main verbs alternate with linking verb–complements to produce the following contrast: change / be the same / change. The pattern of repetition is also advanced within these clauses. The auxiliary "will" is repeated in all three clauses. Then part of the verb phrase ("never change") of the first main clause of sentence 6 is repeated in sentence 8.

Sentence length shows a departure from the earlier pattern. The sentences get progressively longer until we reach sentence 7, which is extremely short and abrupt (eight words). Sentence 8 is also short (eleven words).

Sentences 8 and 9, the first two sentences of the last paragraph, are structurally similar:

The tarantula, the adder, and the asp /
will also never change.

Pain and death /
will always be the same.

On the highest structural level, these sentences are parallel. Both have conjoined subjects, and both have similar verb phrases. In addition, the sentences repeat the pattern of negative–positive alternation.

On a lower level, there are patterns of alternation and repetition. Alternation patterns include adverbial contrasts (never / always) and main verb–linking verb–complement contrasts (change / be the same). Patterns of repetition include the repetition of conjoined subjects and of the auxiliary "will." In relationship to previous sentences, the verb phrase "will always be the same" is an identical repetition of the verb phrases in the main clauses of sentences 2, 5, and 6. It also provides a positive contrast to the negatively stated verb phrases in sentences 1, 4, 6, and 8.

In terms of sentence length, sentence 9 contains eight words compared to the eleven words of sentence 8 and the eight words of sentence 7. The six shortest sentences in the discourse appear successively in groups. The first three sentences contain five, seven, and nine words respectively, displaying a progression in sentence length. Sentences 7, 8, and 9 contain eight, eleven, and eight words respectively, moving from short to longer to short.

Sentence 10, the last sentence in paragraph 5 and the final sentence in the discourse, stands in marked contrast to sentence 9:

Pain and death / will always be the same.

But under the pavements trembling like a pulse,
under the buildings trembling like a cry,
under the waste of time,

under the hoof of the beast above the broken bones of
cities,
there / will be / something growing like a flower, something
bursting from the earth again,
forever deathless,
faithful,
coming into life again like April.

The most obvious difference between these two sentences is one of length: sentence 9 contains eight words, sentence 10 contains fifty-five. Although there seems to be no important new movement in terms of length in this last paragraph, the overall movement from sentence to sentence and from paragraph to paragraph reveals a symmetrical pattern. There is a progressive lengthening of sentences and paragraphs until we get to the last sentence in paragraph 4. Sentence 7, the last sentence of that paragraph, abruptly shifts the movement from long to short, so that the last paragraph is shorter than the preceding one. The five paragraphs therefore move from twenty-one words, to forty-three words, to sixty words, to one hundred words, and then to seventy-four words. Not only is the pattern of ascending and descending order of paragraph length orderly, but so is the symmetry in terms of progressive and decreasing length. The paragraphs progress in multiples of twenty words (twenty-one, forty-three, sixty). The difference between paragraphs 3 and 4 is a multiple of forty (sixty, one hundred), but the difference between paragraphs 4 and 5 is again a multiple of twenty (one hundred, seventy-four). It is as if paragraph 5 had been displaced in terms of absolute symmetry, for a rearrangement of the last two paragraphs gives the following pattern: twenty-one, forty-three, sixty, seventy-four, and one hundred words. Both arrangements are symmetrical. The original pattern is a variation (twenty-one, forty-three, sixty, one hundred, seventy-four words) on the absolute pattern.

There is no evidence of structural parallelism between sentences 9 and 10. Nor are there distinct patterns of repetition. There are, however, patterns of contrast and of negative alternation. The whole of sentence 10 provides a semantic contrast to sentence 9. The contrast may be stated thus: although pain and death are permanent features of human existence, there is always the hope of rebirth, which is an equally permanent feature of life on earth. On the word level, negative–positive alternation includes the following patterns: death / deathless and death / life.

As in previous paragraphs, relationships exist between the last two sentences, but there is nothing that can be described as paragraph movement.

In the context of other sentences, sentence 10 reveals a number of structural relationships. Whereas sentences 4 and 5 contain a large number of front-shifted parallel modifiers, and sentence 6 contains a large number of back-shifted parallel modifiers, the last sentence seems to bring these patterns together. This sentence opens with a series of front-shifted modifiers and ends with a series of back-shifted modifiers. The sentence can thus be considered a concluding sentence as well as the final sentence. For it also brings together the various patterns of repetition which are prevalent throughout the discourse. The word "something," which is repeated twice in this sentence, combines the words "some" and "thing" which are the opening words of the discourse, appearing in the first two sentences. In addition, the word "things" is consistently repeated throughout the whole discourse, so that if we include the variations, the word is repeated three times in compound form (something) and eight times as a separate word. Similarly, the phrase "the earth" is stated in the opening paragraph, repeated in various other sentences, and finally repeated again in the concluding sentence for a total of nine repetitions. Other key words found in the concluding sentence which have been repeated throughout are the following: "will" (nine times), "be" (six times), "again" (four times), "forever" (three times). The last sentence also concludes the pattern of negative–positive alternation which was initiated in the opening sentence. Thus the last sentence is a fitting culmination of the structure of the whole.

Structural Features of the Whole

In the analysis of intersentence relationships, broader patterns of style and meaning begin to emerge which are barely discernible on the sentence level. It becomes evident as we begin to consider the individual sentence in the context of all of the other sentences in the discourse that there are even larger patterns of structure and meaning. What are the structural features of the passage that seem to be characteristic of the whole?

The opening sentence begins negatively: "Some things will never change." The second sentence is a variation on the first: "Some things will always be the same." Because of our previous sentence by sentence and intersentence analyses, we can discern some obvious structural features. First, the larger movement seems to be that of negative–positive alternation. The second sentence is a positive version of the first. The main variation is in the verb phrase: will never change / will always be the same. Second, a parallel movement is that of repetition. The noun phrase subject "Some things" in both sentences is repeated, and the auxiliary "will" is also repeated.

In the second paragraph, the main pattern of negative–positive alternation is advanced, as the sentence base of the fourth sentence provides a positive contrast to the second: "these things will never change." The resultant pattern up to this point is negative / positive / negative. The pattern of repetition is advanced in that the sentence base of the third sentence repeats the negative statement of the opening sentence while varying it slightly. The verb phrases constitute an exact repetition: "will never change." In the subject noun phrase the word "these" is substituted for the word "some." In all three sentences, the word "things" is repeated and so is the auxiliary "will."

In the third paragraph the pattern of negative–positive alternation is advanced still further, with the sentence base of the fifth sentence contrasting with the sentence base of the previous sentence: these things will never change / these things will always be the same. In addition, these sentence bases provide alternate versions of the opening sentences, the main contrasting patterns carried by the verb phrases: will never change / will always be the same. The pattern of repetition is identical in the noun phrase subjects of sentences 4 and 5, "these things," and in the auxiliary "will." At this point, our initial provisional statements about the overall structural movements in the discourse begin to be confirmed. The major structural pattern at this point is that of negative–positive alternation. A parallel movement is that of repetition, including variations on the repetition. Further, the variations are repeated often enough so that they constitute a pattern of repetition themselves.

Sentence 6, the initial sentence in the fourth paragraph, continues the pattern of negative–positive alternation. This sentence contains two main clauses. The first ("All things belonging to the earth will never change") provides a negative contrast to sentence 5 ("these things will always be the same"), and repeats the verb phrase pattern of sentences

1 and 4: "will never change." As in the two previous sentences, there is a substitution in the subject slot: "All things belonging to the earth." This pattern is picked up again in slightly varying form in successive phrases within the same sentence ("all things proceeding from the earth to seasons, all things that lapse and change and come again upon the earth") until it culminates with the second main clause repeating in exact form the pattern of sentence 6: "these things will always be the same." The second clause also provides a contrast to the first clause within the same sentence: "All things . . . will never change / these things will always be the same."

Sentence 7, the last sentence in the fourth paragraph, seems to constitute a major structural change in relation to the previous sentences. Nevertheless, the patterns of negative–positive alternation and of repetition are advanced by means of semantically equivalent clauses and phrases: "Only the earth endures, but it endures forever." The verb phrases "endures" and "endures forever" repeat the positive assertions of the previous sentences ("will always be the same") in semantically equivalent terms. And, as in previous sentences, there is a substitution in the subject slots: "Only the earth," and "it."

The first two sentences (8 and 9) of the last paragraph repeat the patterns of the previous sentences. The pattern of negative–positive alternation is carried by the verb phrases: will also never change / will always be the same. Each of these in turn is a repetition of a pattern in a previous sentence. There is also a substitution in the subject slot in both sentences for the more generally stated subject phrases of the opening sentences. (The phrases "The tarantula, the adder, and the asp" and "Pain and death" are substituted for the phrase "Some things.")

The last sentence in the discourse concludes the patterns of alternation and repetition initiated by the opening sentences. It fits the alternating pattern, yet not in the way the earlier sentences have. The negative–positive contrast is partially shifted out of the verb phrase slot and into the nominal slot:

negative nominal: "the tarantula, the adder, and the asp"
negative nominal: "pain and death"
positive nominal: "something growing"
positive nominal: "something bursting"

A part of the contrast is also carried by the adjectivals: forever deathless

/ coming into life again like April. The word "something" brings together in a single compound the opening words ("some" and "thing")
of the initial sentences of the discourse. And the phrases "forever deathless" and "coming into life again like April" are semantic variations of
the negative–positive contrasts (will never change / will always be the
same) of the opening sentences.

At this point it becomes increasingly clear how closely aspects of
style are related to aspects of structure. The smaller details build up
larger and larger patterns of structure and meaning which culminate in
the structure of the whole. A syntagmatic analysis of the discourse enables us to see these interrelationships more clearly:

I

1 Some things will never change.
1 Some things will always be the same.
   2 Lean down your ear upon the earth, and listen.

2

1 The voice of forest water in the night, a woman's laughter in the
dark, the clean, hard rattle of raked gravel, the cricketing stitch of
midday in hot meadows, the delicate web of children's voices in bright
air—these things will never change.

3

1 The glitter of sunlight on roughened water, the glory of the stars,
the innocence of morning, the smell of the sea in harbors, the feathery
blur and smoky buddings of young boughs, and something there
that comes and goes and never can be captured, the thorn of spring,
the sharp and tongueless cry—these things will always be the same.

4

1 All things belonging to the earth will never change—the leaf, the
blade, the flower, the wind that cries and sleeps and wakes again,
the trees whose stiff arms clash and tremble in the dark, and the
dust of lovers long since buried in the earth—all things proceeding
from the earth to seasons, all things that lapse and change and come
again upon the earth—these things will always be the same, for they

come up from the earth that never changes, they go back into the earth that lasts forever.

1 Only the earth endures, but it endures forever.

5

1 The tarantula, the adder, and the asp will also never change.
1 Pain and death will always be the same.
1 But under the pavements trembling like a pulse, under the buildings trembling like a cry, under the waste of time, under the hoof of the beast above the broken bones of cities, there will be something growing like a flower, something bursting from the earth again, forever deathless, faithful, coming into life again like April.

A paradigmatic analysis reveals the underlying features from a slightly different point of view:

Some things	will never change	
Some things		will always be the same
these things	will never change	
these things		will always be the same
All things belonging to the earth	will never change	
all things proceeding from the earth to seasons		
all things that lapse and change and come again upon the earth		
these things		will always be the same
Only the earth		endures
it		endures forever
The tarantula, the adder, and the asp	will also never change	

Pain and death		will always be the same
something		
growing like		
a flower		
something	forever deathless	coming into life again
bursting from		like April
the earth again		

One of the things the schema does is to make clear the central role of the negative–positive contrast. The passage as a whole proceeds by alternation: negative–positive (never / always), negative–positive (never / always), negative–positive (never / always), negative–positive (only / forever), negative-positive (never / always), negative-positive (the tarantula, the adder, and the asp. . . . pain and death / something growing . . . something bursting).

Another thing that becomes evident when one proceeds from feature to feature is the dynamic nature of the passage. Line 1 leads, by a slight modification, to line 2; line 2, to a slightly altered statement in line 3; line 3 leads to line 4 by a slight modification, and so forth. The modifications of earlier statements lead genetically to later statements, but the later statements, despite the structural similarities, are different, significantly different in what they say. No sentence is a main idea, no idea is repeated. What is repeated throughout is process, process of alternation.

Interpretation and Explanation

At this point in the analysis, all of the descriptive statements have been made on every level of structure. This prepares the way for interpreting the passage and explaining the linguistic features and rhetorical method in terms of that interpretation.

We began our investigation by placing the discourse in a special context. We learned that this is a descriptive passage from a novel, and that it is a stream of consciousness illustration of the meeting of a man and a moment, of a mind ready to arrive at that most difficult of perceptions, the perception of the obvious. The passage conveys the experience of the human organism attaining a very particular perception, and the perception itself is secondary to the attainment of the experience. What is the nature of the experience that George undergoes, and what is the insight that he attains? How do the linguistic features and rhetorical method work to convey this experience?

Fundamental to the rhetoric of the passage is the pattern of negative–positive alternation. Why does the discourse begin with a negative statement? This has to do at one level with an expectation of change. George has heretofore been concerned with change, threatened by it in some way. The context indicates that he has been concerned with the change of self.

George's process of discovery develops gradually. The opening sentences are initial clues: the first sentence makes a negative statement, the second sentence is a positive contrast. The purpose of these opening sentences may be conceived of in terms of several different contexts. At one level the purpose is to initiate a reverie. At another level it is to contrast with subsequent sentences in such a way as to permit the subsequent sentences to signal increasing involvement in the reverie and progressive movement toward epiphany. At another level, though this does not emerge until after the analyses of the higher levels of organization, these sentences begin to signal in very bold lines the elements of the process of the whole section.

Subsequent sentences advance the reverie and the progressive patterns of alternation and repetition. But when we get to the last sentence of the third paragraph, something curious happens. If we juxtapose the opening sentences against the last sentence of paragraph 3, we get the following:

Some things will *never change.   Some things* will *always be the same.*
Only the earth endures.   but *it endures forever.*

This is one of the key moments in the passage. Up to this point, George has failed to understand his experience fully, has failed to perceive it clearly. However, at this point he realizes that change endures for all except *earth,* but that the change is always in process, always the process repeats. The transient temporal being is, by changing, an emblem of a permanent process. Only from a view outside of the process, only by some kind of transcendent mystical perspective can one perceive the permanence. The repetitions and the variations within the repetitions are the means of getting to the fundamental truth. The use of repetition is one of the dominant methods used to achieve such insight, for it is incantatory repetition, more important for what it screens out than for what it adds. It is significant that in the context of the passage Wolfe speaks of George and of the man in the window of the warehouse (who becomes a symbol and a means for George to attain his perception) as screening out all of the surrounding activity. For repetition is an excluding device. It is a means whereby George can escape from the activities of the earth to a view outside the process. And the reverie induced by the incantatory repetition becomes the means of attaining the transcendent mystical perspective, the epiphany of the permanence of life as process.

No sentence in the discourse actually contains this idea. No sentence repeats the main idea throughout. What is repeated is process, the process of alternation. The movement of the whole passage is negative to positive. That's why it begins negatively—so that it can end positively, so that it can communicate the joy of an epiphany. Thus it is not until the very last sentence that George has put away change and death and experienced the epiphany of the permanence of life as process, not until the very last sentence that the truth is unveiled, not until then does he have the joy of illumination, of fulfilled perception which is hinted at but never fully attained until the end.

Summary of Conventions and Generalizations

Once the descriptive statements have been made, the passage interpreted, and the main linguistic features and rhetorical method explained, some tentative generalizations can be put forth.

The first important convention is that of negative–positive alternation. The schema previously presented makes clear the central role of this pattern in the discourse. Negative–positive alternation is a major structural principle which may be applicable to much imaginative description, and which perhaps may be a means of contrasting description and exposition, at least description of this sort, which occurs in a novel and which symbolizes the mental process of a character. Notice that the pattern of negative–positive alternation is developed without the use of a thesis sentence. This kind of sentence is perhaps more appropriate for some kinds of expository writing, but not for this kind of writing. As often happens in nonfiction writing, initial sentences may be clues as to what is to follow. But in this case the initial sentences are clues not to content or meaning, but to process or method. (And that may also be the difference between artful language and expository language in general.) Thus the opening pair of sentences provides *not* a main idea, but a major structural principle, an illustration of the rule according to which each subsequent sentence is phrased and placed. The entire discourse is organized around this major structural principle, for there is structural alternation at every level of syntactic and semantic organization: sentence, clause, phrase, and word.

Another important convention is that of structural repetition. Like the pattern of negative–positive alternation, repetition appears at various levels of structure. First, there is the syntactic repetition and arrangement of clauses and phrases in balanced, parallel order in almost every sentence and in every paragraph. Periodic sentences containing lengthy sequences of short, balanced phrases are repeated at various places in the discourse. Within the longer sentences of the discourse, there is a parallel series of balanced phrases, each containing a sensory image, so that the result is a kind of descriptive catalog of sensory perceptions. These parallel phrases, because they are similar in grammatical structure, reinforce the principle of syntactic repetition, but on a lower level than that of sentences and main clauses. The phrases are of two kinds: appositive noun phrases and adverbial phrases. Front-shifted and back-shifted appositive noun phrases are repeated in balanced parallel order twenty-one times throughout the discourse. The front-shifted adverbial phrases are repeated four times toward the end of the passage. Second, there is a repetition of identical words and phrases throughout the discourse. The repetition is of two kinds: anaphoric repetition, the repetition of identical words and word groups at the beginning of successive phrases or clauses; and extended repetition, word repetition which is carried on at some length and which reappears throughout the passage at various intervals after intervening words have appeared. A few examples of the number of key repeated words should suffice to give some notion of the magnitude of the whole. The word "the" is repeated fifty-seven times; the word "earth" is repeated nine times; the word "things," eight times; the word "change," six times; the word "never," six times; "always," four times; "again," four times; "same," four times; "under," four times; "forever," three times; and so forth. In addition to the syntactic repetition of clauses and phrases and the repetition of identical words and phrases, we can include as a special kind of repetition the repetition of words according to the number of syllables they contain. Of a total of two hundred ninety-eight words in this passage, monosyllabic words are repeated two hundred sixteen times, dissyllabic words are repeated seventy-two times, and trisyllabic words are repeated nine times. Besides these, there is a single word of four syllables. Finally, on the lowest level, there is the repetition of vowel and consonant sounds.

Repetition as a major structural principle seems to have the following uses in imaginative writing of this sort. First, the process of syntactic repetition gives a sense of order, permanence, and stability. In this passage it is as if the syntactic repetition were miming grammatically the insight which is George's epiphany. The repetition thus communicates a sense of the abiding forms of earthly existence. Second, repetition may be used to signal an increasing involvement in reverie and a progressive movement toward an epiphany. Repetition as incantation, repetition as a means of achieving mystical insight, seems to be a characteristic device of much imaginative description. Northrop Frye calls this type of repetition "the hypnotic incantation that through its pulsing dance rhythm, appeals to involuntary physical response, and is hence not far from the sense of magic, or physically compelling power." [14] According to Frye, this kind of repetition shows an underlying pattern of the dream or of the oracular, which in fact we have been referring to as reverie. Third, repetition may be used in imaginative writing to produce a distinctive prose rhythm. In *The Anatomy of Criticism,* Northrop Frye describes a kind of prose which he labels "melos," or musical prose, that corresponds closely to the kind of prose described in this paper: "a tendency to long sentences made up of short phrases and coordinate clauses, to emphatic repetition combined with a driving linear rhythm, to invective, to exhaustive catalogues, and to expressing the process or movement of thought instead of the logical word-order of achieved thought." [15]

The rhythm achieved by the various kinds of syntactic and verbal repetition has several purposes in this passage. It contributes to the musicality of the lines, and thus has an expressive function. It also reinforces the meaning of the lines which deal with the regulated movements of growth and change in life and nature. Nature is characterized by a balance of motions, by recurrence, by regulated movements, and the rhythms of the lines suggest the rhythms of nature. Finally, the rhythm is a source of formal satisfaction: the regularity of the design sets up certain expectations and the gratification of these expectations is appealing. Rhythm has this formal appeal, according to Kenneth Burke, because it is "closely allied with 'bodily' processes. Systole and diastole, alternation of the feet in walking, inhalation and exhalation, up and down, in and out, back and forth, such are the types of distinctly motor experiences 'tapped' by rhythm. Rhythm is so natural to the organism that even a succession of uniform beats will be interpreted as a succession of accented and unaccented beats. The rhythm of a page, in setting up a corresponding rhythm in the body, creates marked degrees of expectancy, or acquiescence." [16]

In addition to the various kinds and uses of repetition, the spatiality of the clausal repetition seems to be a significant rhetorical convention. In writing of any sort, space is time: it takes twice as much time to read ten lines as it does to read five, and (roughly speaking) twice as much time to read 500 words as 250. The arrangement of the repeated negative–positive alternate clauses reveals the following information about space-time: the first two alternates are contiguous; the parts of the second pair are separated by fifty-three words; the halves of the third pair are separated by fifty-seven words; the halves of the fourth pair of alternates, radically different in form from the other three pairs, are contiguous in contiguous sentences; the alternates in the fifth pair, also different, are contiguous in contiguous sentences; and finally, the alternates of the sixth pair, also different, are contiguous in contiguous pairs of sentences. The spatial relations of the alternates are a clue to, a means of representing, of miming, of dramatizing the movement of a character's mind toward insight. This implies the generalization that in description that uses clausal repetition, the spacing of the repetition may be significantly arranged.

Kenneth Burke's discussion of repetitive form in *Counter-Statement* lends convincing support to our discussion of the principle of repetition as it is used in this passage: Burke contends that this formal pattern is one of the basic principles underlying all discourse. According to Burke, the nature of all form can be reduced to five aspects: "progressive form (subdivided into syllogistic and qualitative progression), repetitive form, conventional form, and minor or incidental forms." [17] Of the nature of repetitive form, Burke comments:

Repetitive form is the consistent maintaining of a principle under new guises. It is restatement of the same thing in different ways. . . . A succession of images, each of them regiving the same lyric mood; a character repeating his identity, his "number," under changing situations; the sustaining of an attitude, as in satire; the rhythmic regularity of blank verse; the rhyme scheme of *terza rima*—these are all aspects of repetitive form. By a varying number of details, the reader is led to feel more or less consciously the principle underlying them—he then requires that this principle be observed in the giving of further details. Repetitive form, the restatement of a theme by new details, is basic to any work of art, or to any other kind of orientation, for that matter.[18]

To Burke, forms of discourse "can be said to have a prior existence in the experiences of the person hearing or reading the work of art. They parallel processes which characterize his experiences outside of art."[19] There are therefore no forms of discourse which do not have their origin as forms of experience outside of the mode of discourse. Each work is thus "an individuation of formal principles. Each work re-embodies the formal principles in different subject-matter."[20] If this is true, then the formal principles of repetition and alternation on which this selection is based are deeply rooted in the nature of man and in the world around him. They are universal patterns of experience exemplified in particular works. They may be called universal "because all men, under certain conditions, and when not in mental or physical collapse, are capable of experiencing them."[21] "They arise out of a relationship between the organism and its environment."[22] Thus life itself is a pattern of recurrence, of repetition, of alternation. It is a pattern of rhythmic growth. It is a complex pattern of movements that can be found in people's every working, playing, and dreaming hour.

The movements of man, of other living organisms, of things could be related to the essential rhythms of nature—years, months, days, the beating of the pulse, breathing, menstrual periods, and so on. . . . Man has been conditioned ever since his appearance in the world, and is constituted in all his physiological structure to obey and respond to a "cosmic rhythm" (bound obviously to breathing, cardiac pulsation, to the mysterious rhythms of the universe, alternating like day and night, the tides, the months, etc.).[23]

Clause length and sentence length are also significant conventions in this discourse. The length of the initial clauses (five words and seven words) of the first two sentences is similar to the length of the clauses (each four words) in sentence 7. Between these two groups of clauses the sentences get progressively longer. These clauses, however, are extremely brief. Why? Here again space-time (length) is the clue. In this passage brevity is a clue to movement, signaling initiation, beginning, first of the whole process, then of the climactic epiphany. And this implies the generalization that extreme brevity of clause length is semantically significant.

Finally, sentence length and paragraph length are significant. The sentences and paragraphs get progressively longer until we get to the turning point in the seventh sentence. At that point the sentences begin to vary in length, and the last paragraph decreases in length. The following scheme shows the overall movement:

Paragraph 1:	21 words	Sentence 1:	5 words
		Sentence 2:	7 words
		Sentence 3:	9 words
Paragraph 2:	43 words	Sentence 4:	43 words
Paragraph 3:	60 words	Sentence 5:	60 words
Paragraph 4:	100 words	Sentence 6:	92 words
		Sentence 7:	8 words
Paragraph 5:	74 words	Sentence 8:	11 words
		Sentence 9:	8 words
		Sentence 10:	55 words

The progression in sentence length is arranged in such a way that it signals the beginning of George's experience in the opening lines, builds in intensity until the turning point in line 7, at the point when George begins to understand his experience, and then culminates in the last sentence with the epiphany. Sentence progression thus illustrates the dramatic sense of change and the dawning perception of the fundamental permanence in the process of change. This leads to the generalization that progressive sentence length may be semantically significant in writing of this sort.

So far in this chapter I have been primarily concerned with showing the complex interrelationships that exist between arrangement and style. But as I have previously pointed out, complex relationships also exist between invention and arrangement and between invention and style. Repetition is certainly a major principle of arrangement, yet I know of no rhetoric or composition books in which repetition is handled as a major structural principle. Alternation is simply one kind of repetition which avoids the strict (and often monotonous) formality that regular repetition produces. But repetition has traditionally been more closely associated with style than with arrangement (except in the more superficial sense in which repetition is considered an important transitional device). The techniques of repetition in classical rhetoric (assonance, anaphora, epistrophe, epanalepsis, anadiplosis, antimetabole, polyptoton) are effective stylistic devices for producing a mature style. But as the foregoing analysis shows, these subtilized stylistic elements combine to produce larger structural patterns that we call patterns of arrangement. The pattern that I refer to as positive–negative alternation is one such structural pattern. Repetition, it seems to me, can also be useful as a topic of invention. Restatement and paraphrase, for example, as subcategories of the topic of repetition, can be useful in expanding and refining our knowledge of a particular subject. They define more clearly the subject to be explored; they give added emphasis to an idea. Repetition is not only a useful rhetorical principle; it is also a fundamental principle in nature and in the universe.

Notes

1. Kenneth Burke, *Counter-Statement*, 2nd ed. (Los Altos: Hermes Publications, 1953), p. 140.

2. The discussion of neologisms, parasemy, polysemy, and homophones in the next 4 paragraphs is taken from: Heinz Werner and Bernard Kaplan, *Symbol Formation* (New York: John Wiley & Sons, Inc.), pp. 240–252.

3. Michael Riffaterre, "Stylistic Context," in *Essays on the Language of Literature*, ed. Seymour Chatman and Samuel R. Levin (Boston: Houghton Mifflin Co., 1967), p. 431.

4. Riffaterre, p. 440.

5. Thomas Wolfe, *You Can't Go Home Again* (New York: Harper & Row Publishers, Inc., 1934), p. 45.

6. James R. Bennett, "A Contextual Method for the Description of Prose Styles," in *Prose Style*, ed. James R. Bennett (San Francisco: Chandler Publishing Co., 1971), pp. 224–231.

7. Frank J. D'Angelo, "Imitation and Style," *College Composition and Communication*, XXIV (October 1973), 283–290.

8. Edward P. J. Corbett, "A Method of Analyzing Prose Style with a Demonstration Analysis of Swift's A Modest Proposal" in *Contemporary Essays on Style*, ed. Glen A. Love and Michael Payne (Glenview, Ill.: Scott, Foresman and Co., 1969), pp. 81–98.

9. Francis Christensen, "A Generative Rhetoric of the Sentence" in *The Sentence and the Paragraph* (Champaign, Ill.: NCTE, 1966), pp. 1–7; Walter A. Cook, S. J., *Introduction to Tagmemic Analysis* (New York: Holt, Rinehart, and Winston, Inc., 1969).

10. Francis Christensen, "A Generative Rhetoric of the Paragraph," *College Composition and Communication*, XVI (October 1965), 144–156; Frank J. D'Angelo, "A Generative Rhetoric of the Essay," *College Composition and Communication* (December 1974).

11. Alton Becker, "A Tagmemic Approach to Paragraph Analysis," *College Composition and Communication*, XVI (December 1965), 237–242; Lubomír Doležel, "Toward a Structural Theory of Content in Prose Fiction," in *Literary Style: A Symposium*, ed. Seymour Chatman (London and New York: Oxford University Press, 1971), pp. 95–110; Michael Grady, "A Conceptual Rhetoric of the Composition," *College Composition and Communication*, XXII (December 1971), 348–354; "On Teaching Christensen Rhetoric," *English Journal*, 61 (September 1972), 859–873, 877; Zellig S. Harris, "Discourse Analysis: in *The Structure of Language*, ed. Jerry A. Fodor and Jerrold J. Katz (Englewood Cliffs, N.J.: Prentice-Hall, Inc., 1964), pp. 355–383; William Oliver Hendricks, *Linguistics and the Structural Analysis of Literary Texts* (Ann Arbor, Michigan:

University Microfilms, Inc., 1969), pp. 76–125; Samuel R. Levin, *Linguistic Structures in Poetry* (The Hague: Mouton and Co., 1962); Claude Lévi-Strauss, "The Structural Study of Myth" in *Myth: A Symposium*, ed. Thomas Sebeok (Philadelphia: American Folklore Society, 1955), pp. 53–65; V. Propp, *Morphology of the Folktale*, 2nd ed. (Austin and London: University of Texas Press, 1968); Boris Tomashevsky, "Thematics" in *Russian Formalist Criticism*, trans., and with Introduction by Lee T. Lemon and Marion J. Reis (Lincoln, Nebraska: University of Nebraska Press, 1965), pp. 61–95.

12. Wolfe, p. 44.

13. Wolfe, p. 44.

14. Northrop Frye, *Anatomy of Criticism* (New York: Atheneum, 1966), p. 266.

15. Frye, p. 266.

16. Burke, p. 140.

17. Burke, p. 124.

18. Burke, p. 125.

19. Burke, p. 143.

20. Burke, p. 143.

21. Burke, p. 149.

22. Burke, p. 170.

23. Gillo Dorfles, "The Role of Motion in Our Visual Habits and Artistic Creation" in *The Nature and Art of Motion*, ed. Gyorgy Kepes (New York: George Braziller, 1965), pp. 42–45.

VIII

CONCLUSION

Throughout this book, I have emphasized a number of important points:

1. that invention, arrangement, and style are connected in important ways;

2. that invention continues throughout the composing process and informs every aspect of a discourse;

3. that nonlogical thought processes and nonverbal modes of consciousness deserve greater attention in the study of rhetoric;

4. that the process of differentiation in the context of holistic thinking has important implications for the study of rhetoric;

5. that the overall shape of a discourse is relatively more important than its parts;

6. that we need to know more about linguistic, rhetorical, and conceptual structures of discourse; and

7. that rhetoric is by its very nature interdisciplinary, so that studies in cognitive psychology, psychoneurology, linguistics, psycholinguistics, and literary criticism, for example, might all be brought to bear on rhetorical studies.

Admittedly, I have raised more questions than I could answer. What I am proposing is more in the nature of an outline than a fully realized theory. In an earlier chapter I indicated that my main concern in this book was to set up a theoretical model based on rhetorical competence. However, the schema I have proposed for exploring invention, arrangement, and style will work as much for rhetorical performance as for rhetorical competence. The schema can be used as devices for composing a discourse as well as for analyzing an already composed discourse.

The theory is open-ended and flexible. Both the order and number of topics are tentative. I have put them into an analytic framework to suggest their interrelationships and to indicate that some kind of ordering might be a pedagogical aid to memory. In addition, I have selected only those categories that seem to be related to perceptual and conceptual mental processes and to conceptual patterns of arrangement and style. Further research would add a significant number of new topics and would thereby change the manner in which we perceive their basic relationships. There is also nothing final about the number and kinds of patterns of arrangement, of syntagms or paradigms, or of elements of style, and the linguistic and rhetorical techniques used to describe these patterns are only suggestions.

Implications for Research

Hopefully, this theory will be useful to teachers and scholars. It obviously raises many questions for scholars to pursue. I have mentioned, for example, that we need to know much more about the topics of invention, both logical and non-logical, and about how they are related to each other and to underlying thought processes. We need to know more about the patterns that inform mature instances of extended discourse, and we need exact syntagmatic and paradigmatic analyses and descriptions of these patterns. We need to know the techniques that a writer or speaker uses to achieve a meaningful whole, how words and sentences are arranged in meaningful patterns, and what the rhetorical effects of these patterns may be. We need to be able to identify basic pattern types, to be able to determine how they can be useful to other writers and what the advantages are of using one particular pattern over another in different contexts. We need to know much more about the relationships between style and arrangement, between invention and arrangement, and between invention and style.

We need to know more about form consciousness. For example,

what do recent psycholinguistic studies of a child's acquisition of language have to tell us about concepts of rhetorical form? Can structure be taught explicitly by the teacher or does it have to be discovered by the children themselves? Psycholinguists tell us that children acquire a relatively sophisticated grammar by the time they are six with almost no direct instruction. How is this done? From all outward accounts, the child seems to be observing and imitating abstract language patterns which then become creative in the production of new forms. Observation and imitation. Not of content, but of forms, patterns, structures, grammatical and rhetorical principles. It is not known, however, whether children use in their speech the more complex syntactic forms that are later used in their writing. Psycholinguistics may eventually have much to tell us about form consciousness in children's thinking and writing.

I have previously stated that new insights derived from such disciplines as anthropology, linguistics, psychobiology, speech, literary criticism, sociolinguistics, and biology may be important in generating new research. For example, Edward T. Hall, in his book, *The Hidden Dimension,* makes us aware of the limitations of the treatment of spatial order in traditional (classroom) rhetoric and composition texts. In these books, spatial description is conceived of almost entirely in visual terms. Yet Hall makes it perfectly clear that the perception of space involves not only visual space, but also auditory space, olfactory space, thermal space, and tactile space. Hall's discussion of space suggests new categories for perceiving the ordering of descriptive discourse: distant (eyes, ears, nose) and immediate (skin and muscles) receptors; art as a clue to perception; literature as a key to perception; and proxemics, the theory of humans' use of space as an extension of culture, including the notion of space as a communications medium. Such topics may have important implications for rhetorical theory and practice.[1]

Many of us are naive about concepts as fundamental as the senses and sensory stimuli. In his book, *The Senses,* the biologist Otto Lowenstein outlines a new way of dividing sensory stimuli into categories which correspond to their physical nature. These are the mechanical, the electromagnetic, and the chemical. A much wider range of sensory receptors corresponds to these than to the traditional five senses.

> Sight, the first and foremost of the classical 'five senses' . . .
> constitutes only a very small part of the total spectrum of electro-
> magnetic energy. . . .

The sense of touch and pain as well as the great variety of sensory mechanisms for the control of posture, movement, balance, and finally, for hearing depend on the registration of mechanical deformation of parts of the body situated at the surface or in deeper tissues and in special organs. As heat is physically speaking a mechanical phenomena, the temperature sense, too, will have to be dealt with under this heading. It will be seen that the organs of the temperature sense are in fact closely allied to the organs of touch.

Smell and taste are the chief chemical senses, but as can be expected, animals react to a wider range of chemical agents than those familiar to us through the good offices of our noses and palates, and it will be necessary to consider a general chemical sense in addition to the two classical categories of smell and taste.[2]

The point is that as modern science becomes more and more knowledgeable about the world of nature, about the constitution of matter, and about the human body and personality, new concepts will begin to emerge to explain them. Such new concepts will force us to perceive reality in new ways, for once new categories and principles are acquired and become habitual with us, they in turn become formal categories which can become conceptual principles and patterns which will enable us to look at language in a new way.

From these few examples, it should be clear that much more basic rhetorical research is needed to enlarge our understanding of the composing process. What follows is a suggestion of the kind of focus such research might take. The study of rhetoric should include:

1. The study of the topics of invention and their relationship to underlying logical thought processes.

2. The study of nonlogical thought processes, including the study of nonverbal modes of consciousness.

3. Careful syntagmatic and paradigmatic analyses and descriptions of extended units of discourse to see what kind of structural patterns exists.

4. A study of the structure of paragraphs, not only as discrete entities, but also as functioning parts of longer units of discourse.

5. A study of intersentence relationships.

6. A study of the stylistic context of individual sentences and of the relationship of style to arrangement.

7. A study of conceptual or meaning patterns which transcend the sentence.

8. A study of form "consciousness."

9. A study of the relationship between thought and speech, between thought and writing, and between speech and writing.

10. A treatment of semantic and lexicological aspects of discourse: vocabulary, archaisms, neologisms, dialectisms, the effect of context on the meaning of a word, usage, and so forth.

11. An understanding of the effects of different patterns of discourse.

12. A study of linguistic, rhetorical, and conceptual differentiation.

13. An analysis of the techniques writers use to achieve their purpose.

14. The relationship between writers and their audiences.

15. The relationship between the subject matter of the discourse and the audience.

16. An examination of the rhetorical situation.

17. A study of metalinguistic stylistic elements such as color, synesthesia, and symbolism.

18. A study of prose rhythm.

19. A study of rhetorical patterns in literature.

20. The study of writing as a collection of subdialects or genres or set forms, with particular attention to such forms as essays, political speeches, presidential addresses, advertising, magazine writing, the sports column, editorials, letters to the editor, the best-seller, and so on.

21. A study of the conceptual structures of discourse as they reflect world views.

Let me pause for a moment and give a specific example of a problem for rhetorical research, one which combines item 17, a study of metalinguistic stylistic elements, and item 21, a study of conceptual structures as they reflect world views. In his discussion of color perception, the biologist Otto Lowenstein notes that color discrimination must be of relatively recent origin. He writes:

> It is fascinating to see how the number of names for different colours varies in various languages and language groups, and even among professional groups using the same language. In everyday English we distinguish basically between purple, blue, green, yellow, orange, and red. The Shona, a native tribe in Rhodesia, have only three colour names in their vocabulary, other tribes have only two. We need not go to Africa to find a group of people using only two colour terms. The botanists subdivide flower colours into cyanic and xanthic (blue- and yellow-tinted). This gives us the key to the apparent poverty of some vocabularies. Colour names in such cases are collective names each covering a range of colours, within which distinctions of hue may or may not be made by qualifying adjectives such as poppy-red or cornflower-blue. The old Anglo-Saxons were apparently more interested in brightness than in colour, hence their frequent allusion to gleaming, shadowy, lowering. Sea-waves, the sword-edge, or a helmet would all be 'brun.' 'Wan' was dull, 'dun' was sallow. Only in later writing do green and red appear with connotations of hue. In old English poetry blue is practically non-existent. Violet and orange, which by the way are both descriptive of natural objects, were also absent from the vocabulary in which green, red and yellow were almost the only colour names. The Romans had words for dark or murky, for chestnut colours, for golden-brown, and even the word 'rubidus' usually translated as red, covered the range between red and black. All this has made people think that colour vision as we know it emerged in historical times. . . . Different civilizations focus a different amount of interest on colour and appreciation of hue grows in proportion to needs.[3]

What a wealth of suggestions for the rhetorician, the linguist, the semanticist! Surely one of the tasks of basic rhetorical research is to investigate, for example, the ways that color concepts have been used historically in prose and poetry. Implicit in the above passage is the Sapir-Whorfian hypothesis, the notion that language influences the worldview of its users.

Language is thus a way of experiencing the universe, of conceptualizing color, time, space, action, causality, and so on. All people do not see the world in the same way. Through language we divide and organize experience in different ways. Writing is one of many ways of experiencing reality, and an important one at that.

Equally fascinating is the evolutionary point of view expressed in this passage, a Lamarckian rather than a Darwinian view. Color differentiation, states Lowenstein, "grows in proportion to needs." The possibility that color differentiation is a process which has developed over a period of time is an interesting idea to contemplate. Parallel processes of change exist in other areas, for example, historical linguistics and psycholinguistics. There is historical evidence to show that in the evolution of the English language there was a gradual process of linguistic change, with the syntax showing a greater degree of differentiation as we approach the modern period. English moved from being primarily an inflectional language to a structural language. Certain content words became functional words, and new functional words such as certain auxiliaries appeared to fulfill certain needs. In psycholinguistics, the study of the acquisition of children's language reveals an apparent microcosm of the process of historical or evolutionary differentiation. In the early stages of language acquisition, for example, semantically the child starts from the whole, from a meaningful complex, and only later is it able to differentiate the separate semantic units; only later does it assign meanings to individual words. The process of invention seems to move from intuitively perceived wholes to differentiated parts. From simplicity to complexity. This seems to be the direction in which the evolutionary process is taking us. (Some scientists would argue that there is a reverse movement toward simplicity as well.) Simplicity in complexity. What are the implications of such ideas for the study of rhetoric?

Another possibility for research is suggested by the interdisciplinary nature of rhetoric. Allan Paivio, in his book *Imagery and Verbal Processes,* suggests that "verbal descriptions of concrete situations and events from memory and verbal expressions of the manipulation of spatial concepts are likely to be mediated efficiently by nonverbal imagery, whereas abstract discourse and verbal expressions of abstract reasoning are more likely to be mediated entirely by the verbal system." [4] The assumption is that linguistic and rhetorical meaning is closely tied to imagery, at least for discourse such as description and narration which rely heavily on concreteness.

Paivio contends that children are exposed to imagery and nonverbal processes before they are exposed to language, but that once verbal skills are acquired both verbal and nonverbal mental processes work together to convey meaning, although it is possible to rely more heavily on the one or the other in mediating ideas. Paivio maintains that not only do children acquire a great number of images which form a foundation for language development, but also that there is a kind of syntax to these nonverbal processes. That is, children do not merely perceive static objects, but they also perceive the relationships that obtain between these objects. They perceive action and sequence and cause and effect which are later represented by the function words of the language.[5]

Paivio believes that the deep structure of meaning that linguists such as Chomsky have been trying to get at is really an underlying structure of imagery and that the child's earliest grammar is tied to this imagery. Later, as its thinking processes become more abstract, it is able to manipulate verbal structures abstracted from the imagery. The relationship between verbal processes and nonverbal processes, however, is relative rather than absolute, contends Paivio. Abstract discourse may also involve nonverbal processes such as imagery at some deeper level of consciousness which is not discernible by our conscious awareness. On the other hand, concrete discourse has intraverbal as well as imagistic levels.[6]

Paivio's study suggests that the rhetorician must find ways to probe the relationship between imagery and the structure of discourse. Clearly the verbal system is always involved in the production of discourse, but what role do nonverbal processes play in the composing process? Apparently we need theoretical studies in rhetoric which correspond in part to those of Paivio in psycholinguistics and Rudolf Arnheim in aesthetics and visual thinking to answer some of these questions. Perhaps we need a new thrust in rhetoric which will combine the disciplines of rhetoric and psychology in the same way that linguistics and psychology were combined to form the interdisciplinary field of psycholinguistics. The term psychorhetoric seems awkward, but some such discipline based on the relationships between psychology and rhetoric may be needed.

Implications for Teaching

For the teacher, I would recommend several roles. The first is that of a teacher of theory. In this role, the teacher first explains the theory and then describes the principles, and the student is then expected to put these principles into practice. The student would be taught something about the composing process, for example, how various theorists and creative artists understand the role of conscious and unconscious mental processes in the act of composition. The teacher would also encourage the student to become familiar with various kinds of linguistic, rhetorical, and psychological theories as they relate to composition.

A second role of the teacher is that of experienced guide. In this role as teachers, we will be leading the student inductively through an examination and description of the writing of the best professional writers, but we will also be interested in describing the language of our students to enable us to understand just how the two kinds of writing may differ. To do this we may have to devise our own techniques for describing writing and to frame questions for arriving at helpful rhetorical statements. We need to conduct our students through a close rhetorical analysis of prose and poetry—of essays, fiction, magazine writing of all kinds, newspaper articles, advertising, and so forth. Then perhaps they might be able to use some of their discoveries. Since each type of writing is different, we might conceive of writing as a collection of genres or sub-dialects, and one of our functions would be to teach the different kinds of genres. Where can students go to get the information they need about a particular genre? How can they be led to understand the logic of what they are working with, to be able to understand the structure, the pattern of events, the pattern of ideas, the patterns of language which are basic to the dialect? How can they be encouraged to make generalizations and meaningful statements about rhetoric? In short, another of our roles as teachers of composition would be that of directing the observations and imitations of our students.

The students' role would be similar to that of the teacher. They too would be describers of mature instances of written discourse as well as of their own writing. This assumes for the students a more active role than they are usually given. Rather than merely passively applying the precepts and principles of others, the students will be led to generate their own knowledge by becoming actively involved in the learning process. At first they may depend a bit on the teacher for some direction, but eventually they will take over the leading role. This means that they will be hard at work discovering patterns, relationships, and meaning in written or oral discourse (and by implication, in the world around them).

They will learn to define the problems they may be asked to solve; to ask pertinent questions relating to their solution; to make observations, analyses, and descriptions; to devise ways of classifying their material; to formulate generalizations, and to be able to support their generalizations by verification. Finally, they would be directed to imitate the patterns of discourse they have examined. In brief, the students will be engaged in the discovery or inquiry method of learning.

The emphasis on creative expression and on personal writing in Great Britain and in the United States in recent years suggests additional roles for both teacher and students. This kind of writing seems to be directly related to the contemporary interest in exploring alternate modes of consciousness. The impetus for such exploration seems to derive, at least in part, from Freudian and Jungian psychology and from humanistic and existential approaches to human behavior by such psychologists as Rollo May, Abraham Maslow, Carl Rogers, and R. D. Laing. The importance of these new approaches is that they provide a healthy balance to the rational, systematic approaches to writing which have long dominated the classroom. These new approaches emphasize feeling rather than intellect, exploration and discovery rather than preconceived ideas, the imagination, creativity, free association, fantasy, play, dreams, the unconscious, nonintellectual sensing, the stream-of-consciousness, and the self.

The teacher's role in directing such writing is similar to that of a psychotherapist, accepting the students' writing with all of its imperfections as a direct reflection of their feelings and their self-worth. Fixed forms and propriety in language are anathema. The job of the teacher is to make it easier for the students to communicate their feelings and emotions. As Carl Rogers puts it: *"I have found it enriching to open channels whereby others can communicate their feelings, their private perceptual worlds to me.* Because understanding is rewarding, I would like to reduce the barriers between others and me, so that they can, if they wish, reveal themselves more fully." [7]

This new emphasis on writing which is relatively free of control and direction may be termed the new romanticism. It holds that not all of our mental processes are rational. It denies that the intellect is more in touch with reality than the imagination or other nonlogical processes. Characteristic of this view is a comment by James Miller in his book, *Word, Self, Reality: The Rhetoric of Imagination.* In the opening chapter, Miller presents his premise:

The mystery of language is, in large part, the mystery of the processes of the imagination; indeed, language and imagination are so closely intertwined that it would be impossible to untangle them. Probably there is no use of language that does not involve some part of the imagination. And, conversely, the imagination no doubt finds some of its finest manifestations in language. For too long the assumption has been made that language used by an individual originates in the orderly processes of his rational mind, in his reason, in his faculty of systematic logic. Instruction in language-use has therefore been largely aimed at this logical faculty, in the belief that the teaching of orderly processes will result in good writing. The result, though, has too often been not good writing but dead writing, obedient to all the inhibitions and restraints drilled into the reason, but generally dehumanized and unreadable.[8]

Miller's book abounds in quotations from Abraham Maslow, Norman O. Brown, R. D. Laing, D. T. Suzuki, Carl Jung, Margaret Mead, and others. The juxtaposition of these figures can hardly be called accidental. It reveals a romantic and highly personal view of life and experience so in keeping with the newer views of writing. How does one write according to this view?

Forget all rules, forget all restrictions as to taste, as to what ought to be said, write for the pleasure of it—whether slowly or fast—every form of resistance to a complete release should be abandoned.

For today we know the meaning of depth, it is a primitive profundity of the personality that must be touched if what we do is to have it. The faculties, untied, proceed backward through the night of our unconscious past. It goes down to the ritualistic, amoral past of the race, to fetish, to dream, to wherever the "genius" of the particular writer finds itself able to go. . . .

The demonic power of the mind is its racial and individual past, it is the rhythmic ebb and flow of the mysterious life process and unless this is tapped by the writer nothing of moment can result.[9]

Students can write meaningful prose only if they are allowed complete freedom to assert *their* selves, *their* world views. Writing should not be the imposing of form upon content but rather the adapting of the form to the expression. Such "natural" writing as it has come to be called is deeply rooted in our instinctive nature. This natural and spontaneous view of writing seems to have manifested itself in a variety of approaches being tried out in the United States and Great Britain. Foremost among these approaches is the one based on personal writing espoused by British educators such as John Dixon who writes of his approach:

> In such *personal* writing, as it has come to be called, the teacher is looking for an effort to achieve insight—to brush aside the everpresent invitation to take the world as other people have found it, adopting ready-made their terms and phrases (their image of us). Writing is a way of building a personal world and giving an individual rather than a stereotyped shape to our day-by-day experience. Personal writing has to take feeling as well as thought into account, attitudes as well as observations. Characteristically it uses prose as an undifferentiating matrix that blends discussion of ideas with the sense of felt experience. In its way, then, this is a starting point to which we continually recur.[10]

To those who see the processes of theory and practice and of deduction and induction as being mutually exclusive, I can only answer that one rarely comes to the study of anything with a *tabula rasa*. In the discovery process, one usually proceeds from a knowledge of principles and ideas already known to the discovery of new ones. Thus a prior knowledge of the principles and categories obtained not only from the study of rhetoric, but also from such disciplines as linguistics, psycholinguistics, psychology, philosophy, biology, or modern logic may all play an important part in the discovery process. My notion is that rhetoricians have been bound by traditional categories and ideas for so long that they must deliberately go outside of their own discipline to obtain new ways of perceiving reality and of organizing discourse. Ultimately it is what is on the printed page that matters, observable forms which can be subjected to close examination and verification. But there is no reason why we cannot come to our observations and analyses of written or spoken discourse with new insights derived from theory in rhetoric and in other disciplines.

This study makes no claim to completeness. Its purpose is to present an outline, and to suggest *one* direction that an emerging new rhetoric might take. It recognizes that the processes of scholarly inquiry are perhaps more important than subject matter, and in line with recent educational advances, it suggests new roles for teachers and students in the learning process.

If I seem to be overly optimistic about the possibilities of a new rhetoric, it is because I have been invigorated by the insights which I feel the new sciences will contribute to the study of rhetoric. Linguistics, psycholinguistics, semantics, neuropsychology, psychotherapy, anthropology, biology: the new rhetoricians will range widely in all of these disciplines and in many more. But if new developments in rhetoric are to come to pass, English departments will have to evidence much more interest in rhetorical research than they have done in the past. New projects are needed in basic rhetorical research, pedagogical rhetorical research, and metarhetorical research. Graduate students in English need to know much more about the history of rhetoric, rhetorical theory, and the teaching of writing, and they will need to have much more work in the practice of writing. The intent is not to carve out a niche for rhetoricians in the English departments. Rather the opposite is intended. New advances in education suggest the need for more interdisciplinary studies. Since language is basic to all disciplines, there is no reason why, for example, linguists, psycholinguists, philosophers, and literary critics should not be asked to contribute their scholarship to such an important area of human knowledge. In this age of increasing specialization, rhetoric may be one area where knowledge can be made whole again.

Notes

1. Edward T. Hall, *The Hidden Dimension* (Garden City: Doubleday and Co., Inc., 1966), pp. 1, 37–70.

2. Otto Lowenstein, *The Senses* (Baltimore: Penguin Books, 1966), pp. 16–17.

3. Lowenstein, pp. 80–81.

4. Allan Paivio, *Imagery and Verbal Process* (New York: Holt, Rinehart and Winston, Inc., 1971), p. 434.

5. Paivio, pp. 437–438.

6. Paivio, pp. 438–439.

7. Carl Rogers, *On Becoming a Person* (Boston: Houghton Mifflin Co., 1961), p. 19.

8. James E. Miller, Jr., *Word, Self, Reality: The Rhetoric of Imagination* (New York: Dodd, Mead, & Co., 1972), pp. 3–4.

9. William Carlos Williams, "How to Write," quoted in James E. Miller, Jr., *Word, Self, Reality: The Rhetoric of Imagination.*

10. John Dixon, "Creative Expression in Great Britain," *English Journal*, 57 (September 1968), 797.

A SELECTED
BIBLIOGRAPHY

Rhetoric

Aristotle. *The Rhetoric of Aristotle,* trans. Lane Cooper. New York: Appleton-Century-Crofts, 1960.

Benson, Thomas and Michael H. Prosser. *Readings in Classical Rhetoric.* Bloomington and London: Indiana University Press, 1972.

Booth, Wayne C. "The Revival of Rhetoric." *PMLA,* LXXX (May 1965), 8–12.

Booth, Wayne C. *The Rhetoric of Fiction.* Chicago: The University of Chicago Press, 1961.

Bryant, Donald C., ed. *Papers in Rhetoric and Poetic.* Iowa City: University of Iowa Press, 1965.

Burke, Kenneth. *A Rhetoric of Motives.* Englewood Cliffs, N.J.: Prentice-Hall, Inc., 1950.

Corbett, Edward P. J. *Classical Rhetoric for the Modern Student.* New York: Oxford University Press, 1971.

Corbett, Edward P. J. "What Is Being Revived?" *College Composition and Communication,* XVIII (October, 1967), 166–172.

Corder, Jim W. *Uses of Rhetoric.* New York: J. B. Lippincott Co., 1971.

Douglas, Donald G., ed. *Philosophers on Rhetoric*. Skokie, Ill.: National Textbook Co., 1973.

Ehninger, Douglas. *Contemporary Rhetoric*. Glenview, Ill.: Scott, Foresman and Co., 1972.

Gorrell, Robert M., ed. *Rhetoric: Theories for Application*. Champaign, Ill.: NCTE, 1967.

Gorrell, Robert M. "Very Like a Whale—A Report on Rhetoric." *College Composition and Communication*, XVI (October, 1965), 138–143.

Howell, Wilbur Samuel. *Logic and Rhetoric in England, 1500–1700*. New York: Russell and Russell, Inc., 1961.

Howes, Raymond F., ed. *Historical Studies of Rhetoric and Rhetoricians*. Ithaca, N.Y.: Cornell University Press, 1961.

Hughes, Richard E. "The Contemporaneity of Classical Rhetoric." *College Composition and Communication*, XVI (October, 1965), 157–159.

Joseph, Sister Miriam, C. S. C. *Shakespeare's Use of the Arts of Language*. New York: Columbia University Press, 1947.

Kinneary, James L. *A Theory of Discourse*. Englewood Cliffs, N.J.: Prentice-Hall, Inc., 1971.

Lechner, Sister Joan Marie, O. S. U. *Renaissance Concepts of the Commonplaces*. New York: Pageant Press, Inc., 1962.

Murphy, James J. "The Four Faces of Rhetoric: A Progress Report." *College Composition and Communication*, XVII (May, 1966), 55–59.

Natanson, Maurice and Henry W. Johnstone, Jr., eds. *Philosophy, Rhetoric and Argumentation*. University Park, Penn.: The Pennsylvania State University Press, 1965.

Ohmann, Richard. "In Lieu of a New Rhetoric." *College English*, XXVI (October, 1964), 17–22.

Ong, Walter J., S. J. *The Presence of the Word*. New Haven and London: Yale University Press, 1967.

Ong, Walter J., S. J. *Rhetoric, Romance and Technology*. Ithaca, N.Y.: Cornell University Press, 1971.

Perelman, Chaim and L. Olbrechts-Tyteca. *The New Rhetoric*, trans. John Wilkinson and Purcell Weaver. South Bend, Ind.: University of Notre Dame Press, 1969.

Robinson, James E. *The Scope of Rhetoric*. Glenview, Ill.: Scott, Foresman and Co., 1970.

Sams, Henry W. "Fields of Research in Rhetoric." *College Composition and Communication,* V (May, 1954), 60–65.

Schwartz, Joseph. "Kenneth Burke, Aristotle, and the Future of Rhetoric." *College Composition and Communication,* XVII (December, 1966), 210–216.

Schwartz, Joseph and John A. Rycenga. *The Province of Rhetoric.* New York: The Ronald Press, 1965.

Steinmann, Martin, Jr., ed. *New Rhetorics.* New York: Charles Scribner's Sons, 1967.

Steinmann, Martin, Jr. "Rhetorical Research." *College English,* XXVII (January, 1966), 278–85.

Toulmin, Stephen. *The Uses of Argument.* New York: Cambridge University Press, 1958.

Whipp, Leslie T. "The Language of Rhetoric." *College Composition and Communication,* XIX (February, 1968), 15–21.

Winterowd, W. Ross. *Rhetoric: A Synthesis.* New York: Holt, Rinehart and Winston, Inc., 1968.

Yates, Frances A. *The Art of Memory.* London: Routledge and Kegan Paul, 1966.

Young, Richard E., Alton L. Becker, and Kenneth L. Pike. *Rhetoric: Discovery and Change.* New York: Harcourt Brace Jovanovich, Inc., 1970.

Theory

Black, Max. *Models and Metaphors.* Ithaca, N.Y.: Cornell University Press, 1966.

Bormann, Ernest. *Theory and Research in the Communicative Arts.* New York: Holt, Rinehart, and Winston, 1966.

Bowers, John W. *Designing the Communication Experiment.* New York: Random House, 1970.

Braithwaite, Richard B. *Scientific Explanation.* Cambridge: Cambridge University Press, 1968.

Brockriede, Wayne E. "Toward a Contemporary Aristotelian Theory of Rhetoric." *Quarterly Journal of Speech,* LII (1966), 33–40.

Brody, Baruch A., ed. *Readings in the Philosophy of Science.* Englewood Cliffs, N.J.: Prentice-Hall, Inc., 1970.

Campbell, Karlyn Kohrs. "The Ontological Foundations of Rhetorical Theory." *Philosophy and Rhetoric*, 3 (Spring, 1970), 97–108.

Chomsky, Noam. *Aspects of the Theory of Syntax*. Cambridge, Mass.: The M.I.T. Press, 1965.

Crombie, A. C., ed. *Scientific Change*. New York: Basic Books, Inc., 1963.

Driessel, A. Berkley. "Communications Theory and Research Strategy: A Metatheoretical Analysis." *Journal of Communication*, XVII (June, 1967), 92–107.

Hanson, Norwood Russell. *Patterns of Discovery*. Cambridge: Cambridge University Press, 1958.

Harre, Rom. *The Principles of Scientific Thinking*. Chicago: The University of Chicago Press, 1970.

Holton, Gerald. *Introduction to Concepts and Theories in Physical Science*. Reading, Mass.: Addison-Wesley Publishers, 1962.

Johannesen, Richard L., ed. *Contemporary Theories of Rhetoric: Selected Readings*. New York: Harper and Row, 1971.

Katz, Jerrold L. *The Philosophy of Language*. New York: Harper and Row, 1966.

Kinneary, James L. *A Theory of Discourse*. Englewood Cliffs, N.J.: Prentice-Hall, Inc., 1971.

Kuhn, Thomas S. *The Structure of Scientific Revolutions*. Chicago: The University of Chicago Press, 1962.

Miller, Gerald R. *Speech Communication: A Behavioral Approach*. Indianapolis: Bobbs-Merrill, 1966.

Nagel, Ernest. *The Structure of Science*. New York: Harcourt Brace Jovanovich, Inc., 1961.

Nagel, Ernest, Patrick Suppes, and Alfred Tarski, eds. *Logic, Methodology, and Philosophy of Science*. Menlo Park, Calif.: Stanford University Press, 1962.

Oliver, Robert T. *Culture and Communication*. Springfield, Ill.: Charles C Thomas, 1962.

Pepper, Stephen C. *World Hypotheses*. Berkeley: University of California Press, 1970.

Popper, Karl R. *The Logic of Scientific Discovery*, trans. Julius and Lan V. Fried. London: Hutchinson and Co., 1959.

Smith, Raymond G. *Speech Communication: Theory and Models*. New York: Harper and Row, 1970.

Thayer, Lee. "On Theory-Building in Communication: Some Conceptual Problems." *Journal of Communication,* 13 (December, 1963), 217–235.

Toulmin, Stephen. *The Uses of Argument.* New York: Cambridge University Press, 1958.

Wallace, Karl. *Understanding Discourse: The Speech Act and Rhetorical Action.* Baton Rouge: Louisiana State University Press, 1970.

Weaver, Richard M. *Ideas Have Consequences.* Chicago: University of Chicago Press, 1948.

Weaver, Richard M. *Visions of Order.* Baton Rouge: Louisiana State University Press, 1964.

Wolman, Benjamin B. *Contemporary Theories and Systems in Psychology.* New York: Harper and Row, 1960.

Young, Richard E., Alton L. Becker, and Kenneth L. Pike. *Rhetoric: Discovery and Change.* New York: Harcourt Brace Jovanovich, Inc., 1970.

Invention

Aristotle. *The Rhetoric of Aristotle,* trans. Lane Cooper. New York: Appleton-Century-Crofts, 1960.

Aristotle. *Rhetorica,* trans. W. Rhys Roberts. Oxford: Clarendon Press, 1924.

Bailey, Dudley. "A Plea for a Modern Set of Topoi." *College English,* XXVI (November, 1964), 111–116.

Berthoff, Ann. "The Problem of Problem Solving." *College Composition and Communication,* XXII (October, 1971), 237–242.

Bird, Otto. "The Tradition of the Logical Topics: Aristotle to Ockham." *Journal of the History of Ideas,* 23 (1962), 307–323.

Brake, Robert J. "A Reconsideration of Aristotle's Concept of Topics." *Central States Speech Journal* (May, 1965), 106–112.

Cicero. *De Inventione and Topica,* trans. H. M. Hubbell. London: William Heinemann, Ltd., 1959.

Cicero. *Rhetorica Ad Herennium,* trans. Harry Caplan. London: William Heinemann, Ltd., 1954.

Corbett, Edward P. J. *Classical Rhetoric for the Modern Student.* New York: Oxford University Press, 1971.

Dick, Robert C. "Topoi: An Approach to Inventing Arguments." *Speech Teacher,* 13 (1964), 313–319.

Ehninger, Douglas Wagner. "The Classical Doctrine of Invention." *Gavel,* 39 (1957), 59–62, 70.

Emig, Janet A. *The Composing Processes of Twelfth Graders.* NCTE Research Report No. 13. Urbana, Ill.: NCTE, 1971.

Emig, Janet A. "The Uses of the Unconscious in Composing." *College Composition and Communication,* XV (February, 1964), 6–11.

Harrington, David V. "Teaching Students the Art of Discovery." *College Composition and Communication,* XIX (February, 1968), 7–14.

Harrington, Elbert. "A Modern Approach to Invention." *Quarterly Journal of Speech,* 48 (December, 1962), 373.

Howell, Wilbur Samuel. *Logic and Rhetoric in England, 1500–1700.* New York: Russell and Russell, Inc., 1961.

Jennings, E. M. "A Paradigm for Discovery." *College Composition and Communication,* XIX (October, 1968), 192–200.

Joseph, Sister Miriam, C. S. C. *Shakespeare's Use of the Arts of Language.* New York: Columbia University Press, 1947.

Knapp, Mark and James McCroskey. "The Siamese Twins: Invention and Disposition." *Today's Speech,* 14 (April, 1966), 17–18.

Kytle, Ray. "Prewriting by Analysis." *College Composition and Communication,* XXI (December, 1970), 380–385.

Larson, Richard L. "Discovery Through Questioning: A Plan for Teaching Rhetorical Invention." *College English,* XXX (November, 1968), 126–134.

Larson, Richard. "Invention Once More: A Role for Rhetorical Analysis." *College English,* 32 (March, 1971), 665–672.

Lauer, Sister Janice. "Heuristics and Composition." *College Composition and Communication,* XXI (December, 1970), 396–404.

Lechner, Sister Joan Marie, O. S. U. *Renaissance Concepts of the Commonplaces.* New York: Pageant Press, Inc., 1962.

Nadeau, Ray. "An Analysis of the Commonplaces." *Quarterly Journal of Speech,* 49 (1963), 328–331.

Nelson, William F. "Topoi: Evidence of Human Conceptual Behavior." *Philosophy and Rhetoric,* 2 (Winter, 1969), 1–11.

Ong, Walter J., S. J. *The Presence of the Word.* New Haven and London: Yale University Press, 1967.

Yates, Frances A. *The Art of Memory.* London: Routledge and Kegan Paul, 1966.

Thinking and Consciousness

Alexander, Hubert G. *Language and Thinking.* New York: D. Van Nostrand Co., Inc., 1967.

Arnheim, Rudolf. *Visual Thinking.* London: Faber and Faber, Limited, 1969.

Assagioli, Roberto. *Psychosynthesis.* New York: The Viking Press, 1965.

Berlyne, D. E. *Structure and Direction in Thinking.* New York: John Wiley and Sons, Inc., 1965.

Brassecu, Sabert. "Creativity and the Dimensions of Consciousness." *Humanitas,* 4 (1968), 133–144.

Bruner, Jerome. *On Knowing.* Cambridge: The Belknap Press, 1963.

Freud, Sigmund. *The Interpretation of Dreams,* trans. A. A. Brill. New York: The Modern Library, 1950.

Fromm, Erich. *The Forgotten Language.* New York: Holt, Rinehart, and Winston, Inc., 1957.

Furth, Hans G. *Thinking Without Language.* New York: The Free Press, 1966.

Garma, Ángel. *The Psychoanalysis of Dreams.* Chicago: Quadrangle Books, 1966.

Gazzaniga, Michael S. *The Bisected Brain.* New York: Appleton-Century-Crofts, 1970.

Ghiselin, Brewster. *The Creative Process.* Berkeley and Los Angeles: University of California Press, 1952.

Gibson, J. J. *The Senses Considered as Perceptual Systems.* Boston: Houghton Mifflin Co., 1966.

Gorrell, Robert M. "Structure in Thought." *College English,* 24 (May, 1963), 591–598.

Gutheil, Emil A. *The Handbook of Dream Analysis.* New York: Liveright Publishing Corp., 1951.

Hall, Edward T. *The Hidden Dimension.* Garden City: Doubleday and Co., Inc., 1966.

Hebb, D. O. *The Organization of Behavior.* New York: John Wiley & Sons, Inc., 1949.

Huttenlocker, Janellen. "Constructing Spatial Images: A Strategy in Reasoning." *Psychological Review,* 75 (1968), 550–560.

Inhelder, Barbel and Jean Piaget. *The Growth of Logical Thinking,* trans. Anne Parsons and Stanley Milgram. New York: Basic Books, Inc., 1958.

Jung, C. G. *Psyche and Symbol,* ed. Violet DeLaszlo. New York: Doubleday Anchor Books, 1958.

Koffka, Kurt. *Principles of Gestalt Psychology.* New York: Harcourt, Brace and Co., 1935.

Köhler, Wolfgang. *Gestalt Psychology.* New York: Liveright Publishing Corp., 1947.

Laffal, Julius. *Pathological and Normal Language.* New York: Atherton Press, 1965.

Lowenstein, Otto. *The Senses.* Baltimore: Penguin Books, 1966.

Mandler, J. and G. Mandler, eds. *Thinking: From Association to Gestalt,* New York: John Wiley and Sons, Inc., 1964.

Masters, R. E. L. and Jean Houston. *The Varieties of Psychedelic Experience.* New York: Holt, Rinehart and Winston, 1969.

Miller, Irving Elgar. *The Psychology of Thinking.* New York: The Macmillan Co., 1917.

Naranjo, Claudio and Robert E. Ornstein. *On the Psychology of Meditation.* New York: Viking Press, 1971.

Neisser, Ulric. *Cognitive Psychology.* New York: Appleton-Century-Crofts, 1967.

Neumann, Erich. *The Origins and History of Consciousness,* foreward C. G. Jung, trans. R. F. C. Hull. New York: Pantheon Books, 1954.

Ornstein, Robert E. "Right and Left Thinking." *Psychology Today* (May, 1973), 87–92.

Paivio, A. *Imagery and Verbal Processes.* New York: Holt, Rinehart and Winston, 1971.

Piaget, Jean. *The Psychology of Intelligence,* trans. Malcolm Piercy and D. E. Berlyne. London: Routledge and Kegan Paul, 1951.

Progoff, Ira. *Depth Psychology and Modern Man.* New York: The Julian Press, Inc., 1959.

Progoff, Ira. "The Role of Parapsychology in Modern Thinking," in *The Psychic Force,* ed. and intro. Allan Angoff. New York: G. P. Putnam's Sons, 1970, pp. 49–67.

Rignano, Eugenio. *The Psychology of Reasoning.* New York: Harcourt, Brace & Co., Inc., 1923.

Sokolov, A. N. *Inner Speech and Thought*, trans. George T. Onischenko. New York and London: Plenum Press, 1972.

Sudre, René. *Parapsychology*, trans. C. E. Green. New York: The Citadel Press, 1960.

Tart, Charles T., ed. *Altered States of Consciousness*. New York: John Wiley and Sons, Inc., 1969.

Teilhard de Chardin, Pierre. *The Future of Man*, trans. Norman Denny. New York: Harper Torchbooks, 1964.

Teilhard de Chardin, Pierre. *The Phenomenon of Man*, intro. Sir. Julian Huxley. New York: Harper Torchbooks, 1959.

Vinacke, W. Edgar. *The Psychology of Thinking*. New York: McGraw-Hill, 1952.

Voss, James F., ed. *Approaches to Thought*. Columbus, Ohio: Charles E. Merrill Publishing Co., 1969.

Vygotsky, L. S. *Thought and Language*. Cambridge, Mass.: The M.I.T. Press, 1962.

Werner, Heinz and Bernard Kaplan. *Symbol Formation*. New York: John Wiley and Sons, Inc., 1963.

Wertheimer, Max. *Productive Thinking*, ed. Michael Wertheimer. New York: Harper and Brothers, Publishers, 1959.

West, L., ed. *Hallucinations*. New York: Grune & Stratton, 1962.

Arrangement, Form, and Structure

Abbott, Kenneth M. "Rhetoric and Latin Literary Forms." *Quarterly Journal of Speech,* 36 (1950), 457–461.

Alexander, Christopher. *Notes on the Synthesis of Form*. Cambridge, Mass.: Harvard University Press, 1964.

Arnheim, Rudolf. *Art and Visual Perception*. Berkeley: University of California Press, 1954.

Becker, Alton. "A Tagmemic Approach to Paragraph Analysis." *College Composition and Communication,* XVI (December, 1965), 237–242.

Burke, Kenneth. *Counter-Statement,* 2nd ed. Los Altos, Calif.: Hermes Publications, 1953.

Carrino, Elnora. "Conceptions of Dispositio in Ancient Rhetoric." Unpublished Ph.D. Dissertation. Ann Arbor: University of Michigan, 1959.

Christensen, Francis. "A Generative Rhetoric of the Paragraph." *College Composition and Communication*, XVI (October, 1965), 144–156.

Clarke, Martin L. "The Thesis in the Roman Rhetorical Schools of the Republic." *Classical Quarterly*, 45 (1951), 159–166.

Corbett, Edward P. J. "Arrangement of Material," in *Classical Rhetoric for the Modern Student*, 2nd ed. New York: Oxford University Press, 1971, pp. 299–413.

Cummings, D. W., John Herum, and E. K. Lybbert. "Semantic Recurrence and Rhetorical Form." *Language and Style*, 4 (1971), 195–207.

D'Angelo, Frank J. "A Generative Rhetoric of the Essay." *College Composition and Communication*, XXVII (December, 1974).

Doležel, Lubomír. "Toward a Structural Theory of Content in Prose Fiction," in *Literary Style: A Symposium*, ed. Seymour Chatman. London and New York: Oxford University Press, 1971.

Focillon, Henri. *The Life of Forms in Art*, trans. Charles Beecher Hogan and George Kubler. New Haven: Yale University Press, 1942.

Frank, Joseph. "Spatial Form in Modern Literature," in *Criticism: The Foundations of Modern Literary Judgment*, eds. Mark Schorer, Josephine Miles, and Gordon McKenzie. New York: Harcourt, Brace and World, Inc., 1948, 379–392.

Gibson, James J. *The Perception of the Visual World*. Boston: Houghton Mifflin Co., 1950.

Gibson, J. J. "What Is a Form?" *Psychological Review*, 58 (1951), 403–412.

Grady, Michael. "A Conceptual Rhetoric of the Composition." *College Composition and Communication*, XXII (December, 1971), 348–354.

Grady, Michael. "On Teaching Christensen Rhetoric." *English Journal*, 61 (September, 1972), 859–873, 877.

Harris, Zellig S. "Discourse Analysis," in *The Structure of Language*, eds. Jerry A. Fodor and Jerrold J. Katz. Englewood Cliffs, N.J.: Prentice-Hall, Inc., 1964, pp. 355–383.

Hendricks, William O. "Folklore and the Structural Analysis of Literary Texts." *Language and Style*, 3 (Spring, 1970), 83–121.

Hendricks, William O. *Linguistics and the Structural Analysis of Literary Texts*. Ann Arbor: University Microfilms, Inc., 1969.

Hendricks, William O. "On the Notion 'Beyond the Sentence.'" *Linguistics*, 37 (December, 1967), 12–51.

Kepes, Gyorgy, ed. *Education of Vision.* New York: George Braziller, 1965.

Kepes, Gyorgy, ed. *Structure in Art and in Science.* New York: George Braziller, 1965.

Knapp, Mark and James McCroskey. "The Siamese Twins: Inventio and Dispositio." *Today's Speech,* 14 (April, 1966), 17–18.

Koch, Walter A. "Preliminary Sketch of a Semantic Type of Discourse Analysis." *Linguistics,* 12 (March, 1965), 5–30.

Levin, Samuel R. *Linguistic Structures in Poetry.* The Hague: Mouton and Co., 1962.

Lévi-Strauss, Claude. "The Structural Study of Myth," in *Myth: A Symposium,* ed. Thomas Sebeok. Philadelphia: American Folklore Society, 1955, pp. 53–65.

Parker, John P. "Some Organizational Variables and Their Effect Upon Comprehension." *Journal of Communication,* 12 (March, 1962), 27–32.

Propp, V. *Morphology of the Folktale,* 2nd ed. Austin and London: University of Texas Press, 1968.

Rodgers, Paul, Jr. "A Discourse-Centered Rhetoric of the Paragraph." *College Composition and Communication,* XVII (February, 1966), 2–11.

Rodgers, Paul, Jr. "The Stadium of Discourse." *College Composition and Communication,* XVIII (October, 1967), 178–185.

Tomashevsky, Boris. "Thematics," in *Russian Formalist Criticism,* trans. and intro. Lee T. Lemon and Marion J. Reis. Lincoln: University of Nebraska Press, 1965.

Wells, Rulon. "Is a Structural Treatment of Meaning Possible?" *Proceedings of the Eighth International Conference of Linguists.* Oslo: Oslo University Press, 1958.

Whyte, Lancelot Law. *Accent on Form.* New York: Harper and Brothers, Publishers, 1954.

Whyte, Lancelot Law, ed. *Aspects of Form.* New York: American Publishing Co., Inc., 1968.

Whyte, Lancelot Law, Albert G. Wilson, and Donna Wilson, eds. *Hierarchical Structures.* New York: American Elsevier Publishing Co., Inc., 1969.

Winterowd, W. Ross. "Dispositio: The Concept of Form in Discourse." *College Composition and Communication,* XXII (February, 1971), 39–45.

Winterowd, W. Ross. "New Rhetoric: Form," in *Rhetoric: A Synthesis.* New York: Holt, Rinehart and Winston, Inc., 1968, pp. 117–152.

Young, Richard E., Alton L. Becker, and Kenneth L. Pike. "Writer and Reader: Strategies for Change, Part One and Two," in *Rhetoric: Discovery and Change*. New York: Harcourt Brace Jovanovich, Inc., 1970, pp. 229–290.

Style

Abel, D. Herbert. "Paradox or Oxymoron." *Classical Bulletin*, 34 (1957), 23.

Adolph, Robert. *The Rise of Modern Prose Style*. Cambridge, Mass.: The M.I.T. Press, 1968.

Alonzo, Amado. "The Stylistic Interpretation of Literary Texts." *Modern Language Notes*, LVII (1942), 489–496.

Babb, Howard S., ed. *Essays in Stylistic Analysis*. New York: Harcourt Brace Jovanovich, Inc., 1972.

Bailey, Richard W. "Current Trends in the Analysis of Style." *Style*, I (1967), 1–14.

Bailey, Richard W. and Dolores M. Burton, S. N. D. *English Stylistics: A Bibliography*. Cambridge, Mass. and London: The M.I.T. Press, 1968.

Bennett, James R., ed. *Prose Style: A Historical Approach through Studies*. San Francisco: Chandler Publishing Co., 1971.

Candelaria, Frederick, ed. *Perspectives on Style*. Boston: Allyn and Bacon, Inc., 1968.

Chatman, Seymour, ed. *Literary Style: A Symposium,* trans. in part, Seymour Chatman. London and New York: Oxford University Press, 1971.

Chatman, Seymour and Samuel R. Levin, eds. *Essays on the Language of Literature*. Boston: Houghton Mifflin Co., 1967.

Christensen, Francis. *Notes Toward a New Rhetoric*. New York: Harper and Row, 1967.

Corbett, Edward P. J. "A Method of Analyzing Prose Style with a Demonstration Analysis of Swift's 'A Modest Proposal,'" in *Contemporary Essays on Style,* ed. Glen A. Love and Michael Payne. Glenview, Ill.: Scott, Foresman and Co., 1969.

Corbett, Edward P. J., ed. *Rhetorical Analyses of Literary Works*. New York: Oxford University Press, 1969.

Corbett, Edward P. J. "Style." *Classical Rhetoric for the Modern Student,* 2nd ed. New York: Oxford University Press, 1971.

Crystal, David and Derek Davy. *Investigating English Style*. London and Harlow: Longmans, Green and Co., Ltd., 1969.

Cunningham, J. V., ed. *The Problem of Style*. New York: Fawcett Premier Books, 1966.

D'Angelo, Frank J. "Imitation and Style." *College Composition and Communication*, XXIV (October, 1973), 283–290.

Darbyshire, A. E. *A Grammar of Style*. New York and London: Seminar Press.

Doležel, Lubomír and Richard W. Bailey, eds. *Statistics and Style*. New York: American Elsevier Publishing Co., Inc., 1969.

Eastman, Richard M. *Style: Writing as the Discovery of Outlook*. New York: Oxford University Press, 1970.

Fowler, Roger, ed. *Essays on Style and Language*. London: Routledge and Kegan Paul, 1966.

Freeman, Donald C. *Linguistics and Literary Style*. New York: Holt, Rinehart and Winston, 1970.

Garvin, Paul L., ed. *A Prague School Reader on Esthetics, Literary Structure, and Style*. Washington, D. C.: Georgetown University Press, 1964.

Gibson, Walker. *Persona*. New York: Random House, 1969.

Gray, Barbara B. *Style: The Problem and the Solution*. New York: Humanities Press, 1970.

Hatzfeld, H. A. *A Critical Bibliography of the New Stylistics Applied to the Romance Literatures 1953–1965*. Chapel Hill: University of North Carolina Press, 1966.

Hendricks, William O. "Folklore and the Structural Analysis of Literary Texts." *Language and Style*, 3 (1970), 83–121.

Hendricks, William O. *Linguistics and the Structural Analysis of Literary Texts*. Unpublished Ph.D. Dissertation. University of Illinois, 1965.

Hill, Archibald. "An Analysis of 'The Windhover': An Experiment in Structural Method." *PMLA*, LXX (1955), 968–78.

Hornstein, L. H. "Analysis of Imagery: A Critique of Literary Method." *PMLA*, 57 (1942), 638–53.

Kaplan, Milton. "Style Is Content." *English Journal*, 57 (1968), 1330–34.

Klein, Sheldon. "Control of Style with a Generative Grammar." *Language*, XLI (1965), 619–631.

Koch, Walter Alfred. "On the Principles of Stylistics." *Lingua*, XII (1963), 411–422.

Leech, Geoffrey N. *English in Advertising: A Linguistic Study of Advertising in Great Britain*. London: Longman's, 1966.

Leed, Jacob, ed. *The Computer and Literary Style*. Kent, Ohio: Kent State University Press, 1966.

Levin, Samuel R. *Linguistic Structures in Poetry*. The Hague: Mouton and Co., 1962.

Lodge, David. *Language of Fiction*. New York: Columbia University Press, 1966.

Love, Glen A. and Michael Payne, ed. *Contemporary Essays on Style*. Glenview, Ill.: Scott, Foresman and Co., 1969.

Macksey, Richard and Eugenio Donato, eds. *The Languages of Criticism and the Sciences of Man: The Structuralist Controversy*. Baltimore: The Johns Hopkins Press, 1970.

McIntosh, Angus and M. A. K. Halliday. *Patterns of Language*. Bloomington and London: Indiana University Press, 1966.

Miles, Josephine. *Eras and Modes in English Poetry*. Berkeley and Los Angeles: University of California Press, 1957.

Milic, Louis T. "Metaphysics in the Criticism of Style." *College Composition and Communication*, XVII (October, 1966), 124–29.

Milic, Louis T. *A Quantitative Approach to the Style of Jonathan Swift*. The Hague: Mouton and Co., 1967.

Milic, Louis T. *Style and Stylistics: An Analytical Bibliography*. New York: The Free Press, 1967.

Morse, J. Mitchell. *Matters of Style*. Indianapolis and New York: Bobbs-Merrill, 1968.

Murray, Roger. "A Case for the Study of Period Styles." *College English*, 33 (November, 1971), 139–148.

Ohmann, Richard. "Generative Grammars and the Concept of Linguistic Style." *Word*, 20 (1964), 423–39.

Ohmann, Richard. "Literature as Sentences." *College English*, XXVII (1966), 261–267.

Ohmann, Richard M. *Shaw: The Style and the Man*. Middletown, Conn.: Wesleyan University Press, 1962.

Osborn, Michael. "Archetypal Metaphor in Rhetoric: The Light–Dark Family," in *Contemporary Rhetoric*, ed. Douglas Ehninger. Iowa City: The University of Iowa Press, 1972.

Osborn, Michael. "The Evolution of the Theory of Metaphor in Rhetoric." *Western Speech*, XXXI (Spring, 1967), 121–130.

Rayment, Charles Sanford. "Functional Parallelism in Ancient Rhetoric." *Classical Bulletin*, 25 (1949), 21–22.

Reid, Ronald F. "Books: Some Suggested Reading on the History of Ancient Rhetorical Style." *Central States Speech Journal*, II (1960), 116–122.

Roberts, Thomas J. "Literary-Linguistics: A Bibliography, 1946–1961." *Texas Studies in Literature and Language*, IV (1962), 625–629.

Robinson, James E. "Style." *The Scope of Rhetoric*. Glenview, Ill.: Scott, Foresman and Co., 1970.

Saha, P. K. "A Linguistic Approach to Style." *Style*, 2 (1968), 7–31.

Sebeok, Thomas A., ed. *Style in Language*. Cambridge, Mass.: The M.I.T. Press, 1960.

Sledd, James. "Coordination (Faulty) and Subordination (Upside-down)." *College Composition and Communication*, VII (December, 1956), 181–187.

Sontag, Susan. "On Style." *Partisan Review*, XXXII (1965), 543–560.

Spencer, John, ed. *Linguistics and Style*. London: Oxford University Press, 1965.

Steinmann, Martin, Jr., ed. *New Rhetorics*. New York: Charles Scribner's Sons, 1967.

Strelka, Joseph, ed. *Patterns of Literary Style*. University Park: Pennsylvania State University Press, 1971.

Thomas, Owen. *Metaphor and Related Subjects*. New York: Random House, 1969.

Tufte, Virginia. *Grammar as Style*. New York: Holt, Rinehart and Winston, Inc., 1971.

Ullmann, Stephen. *Meaning and Style*. Oxford: Basil Blackwell, 1973.

Wermouth, Paul C. *Modern Essays on Writing and Style*, 2nd ed. New York: Holt, Rinehart and Winston, Inc., 1969.

Wimsatt, W. K., Jr. *The Verbal Icon*. New York: The Noonday Press, 1962.

INDEX